Prais

"This wry, surprising, nimble book—allergic to genre labels, and positively vibrating with insight—achieves what only great art can manage: to be both impossible to imagine, and utterly necessary. I was absolutely spellbound."
—Leslie Jamison, author of *Splinters*

"A singular, bewitching work about cycles of life and loss, the patterns of behavior that seem to lock us into who we are, and the quest for a faith that might break us free."
—Hua Hsu, author of *Stay True*

"A brilliantly innovative memoir-cum-novel that unsettles and enthralls. As Catherine Lacey navigates a winding path of loss and self-discovery, she meditates on spirituality, the illusion of safety, the nature of art, and the transformative power of rupture; the result is a meditation of startling immediacy and depth."
—Meghan O'Rourke, author of *The Invisible Kingdom*

THE MÖBIUS BOOK

THE MÖBIUS BOOK

CATHERINE LACEY

FARRAR, STRAUS AND GIROUX • NEW YORK

Farrar, Straus and Giroux
120 Broadway, New York 10271

Printed in the United States of America
First edition, 2025

Title-page art by Foto-Ruhrgebiet / Shutterstock.com.

Library of Congress Cataloging-in-Publication Data
Names: Lacey, Catherine, 1985– author.
Title: The Möbius book / Catherine Lacey.
Description: First edition. | New York : Farrar, Straus and
Giroux, 2025. Bound together back-to-back and inverted
(tête-bêche), each with its own title page.
Identifiers: LCCN 2024053381 | ISBN 9780374615406 (hardcover)
Subjects: LCSH: Lacey, Catherine, 1985– | LCGFT: Fiction. |
Creative nonfiction.
Classification: LCC PS3612.A335 M63 2025 | DDC 813/.6—
dc23/eng/20250131
LC record available at https://lccn.loc.gov/2024053381

Designed by Gretchen Achilles

Our books may be purchased in bulk for promotional,
educational, or business use. Please contact your local bookseller
or the Macmillan Corporate and Premium Sales Department at
1-800-221-7945, extension 5442, or by email at
MacmillanSpecialMarkets@macmillan.com.

www.fsgbooks.com
Follow us on social media at @fsgbooks

1 3 5 7 9 10 8 6 4 2

This is a work of nonfiction. However, the author has used
pseudonyms for a couple of individuals to protect their privacy
and has reconstructed dialogue to the best of her recollection.

Para las dos Brendas

THE MÖBIUS BOOK

O dd impulse to catalog these days, not that I can forget them, not that I can remember them clearly.

I woke in the guest room, the attic, a guest in my own home. I'd never slept a night in that room, and staring up at the white clapboard ceiling and walls, I felt I'd been shrunk down and shoved into a doll's house, and I knew then—again, or for the first time—how grief expands as it constricts, how it turns a person into a toy version of herself.

A man downstairs was The Reason I'd turned from inhabitant to visitor.

My phone rang. The Reason was calling me from the floor below. He wanted to know if I would say goodbye to him before I went to the airport.

What have I been doing all week, I asked, *if not saying goodbye to you?*

I hung up.

Before we bought that house, when we lived in Berlin, The Reason bought me an unreasonably expensive Japanese teacup. I felt the teacup was too nice to own, feared I would break it, and The Reason often brought up the fact that I did not use the Japanese teacup often enough, that I obviously did not appreciate the teacup's beauty or The Reason's generosity, but I thought I did appreciate that beauty, that generosity, and occasionally I told him so, but The Reason insisted I did not, that I could not possibly feel appreciative based on my behavior vis-à-vis the teacup, so I began to think he was probably right, and I put my hopes toward truly becoming the person for whom this teacup had been intended, someone who used it with frequency and pleasure, a person who didn't feel guilty about being given something so costly that she did not, perhaps, deserve, and I hoped to become this deserving person very soon, at some reachable point in the foreseeable future.

One afternoon during the days I lived as a guest in my home, I returned from a walk in the cold to find The Reason sitting silent in the living room. I took the Japanese teacup from the cupboard, set it on the floor, took a hammer from the tool closet, and set it beside the teacup.

You have to break it, I told him, and after some hesitation, he did.

The beautiful woman smiled as she told us the story of her grandmother, who had also been beautiful, a woman who had come of age in postwar Greece, knowing hunger, knowing fear intimately. But everything worked out in the end. She survived those desperate years, married, had children, raised children, saw those children have children, and everyone was beautiful.

Recently this woman had asked her grandmother what she would do if she was single and young again and had to marry either a very beautiful man who was evil or a very ugly man who was kind. The grandmother was unapologetic and unequivocal in her answer—evil beauty—which proved the grandmother's tenacious vanity, the beautiful woman explained.

But it made sense, I said, *given her childhood, the war, the things she'd lived through.* To me it seemed clear that evilness is just extreme self-preservation, and to be his possession would accompany his protection.

Now I have to revise the whole way I saw her, she said, laughing, and the conversation took over the table: the evil-beauty and ugly-kindness dichotomy. Everyone's charming, tipsy opinions. The couple on my left was newly in love, and the man on my right was heartbroken, and everyone was dressed up, as our friends had just married in a garden flush with new flowers. I didn't say anything else on the matter, but I could feel the ease of the grandmother's decision so clearly; it likely wasn't Hitler-evil she was imagining in this hypothetical husband, but an average, domestic sort, the kind that's more Machiavellian than sadistic, a man who can make you feel he knows you better than you know yourself, and oh, how nice it is to feel known.

Several seasons after those days in the guest room, I found myself living an unexpected life in a different country. When my new friend, Robin, asked if I was writing another novel, I surprised myself when I said, *I don't want to write fiction anymore. I'm tired of being punked.*

We both laughed, and she asked what I meant, and I told her that nearly every time I've written a novel something happens in between its completion and its publication that makes it clear to me that I knew something I didn't know I knew while I was writing, and that buried knowledge, that unknown known, has been expressed in the fiction, without my awareness. What I think I'm doing when I write a novel and what I later realize I've done is so out of sync that I've felt repeatedly shocked and sometimes embarrassed at how I've tricked myself once again. Robin smiled darkly. Certainly her work as a poet and a translator had put her in touch with the many strange undertows that can develop beneath the surface of a text.

My friend Heidi's son once told her he wasn't going to finish reading a book he'd begun. *What's wrong with the book?* she asked. *Too fictiony*, he said. *What do you mean, too fictiony?* she asked. *Too realistic*, he said.

But I know I'm not done. I feel sure I'll be punked again, because I hate writing fiction with the equal and opposite force of how much I love it. What a stupid, wonderful way to waste my life.

The last time Lozano was brokenhearted she laid in bed staring at NASA photographs—impossible things in the dark, neon planets or milky nebulas or just space, just huge spaces of space.

She had visited me briefly in Chicago then, where I lived with The Reason, and now I was on her doorstep in Escandón, the first of January, swapping roles in this eternal return of disruption, taking care and being taken care of like that hundred dollars passed between broke friends, finding whomever needs it the most at the moment. Hello, life—this is your old life calling.

I spent mornings in her apartment going through copyedits of the last novel I wrote while living with The Reason: *I fear I am the sort of person who needs to feel some measure of fear in order to love someone,* my old self had written, pretending to be someone else. *Well that can't be good,* I tell her, too late.

Months pass, the copyedits are done, the book's gone to press, then Lozano asks what I'm writing about now. I tell her I'm writing about this.

Which this? This-this? she asks.

Yes, I say, *this, my confusion, my friends, self-betrayal, losing faith then gaining it again. The way a story comes back to retell itself.*

OK, she says, *just make me four inches taller.* And it's then that it occurs to me—no one ever notices how Lozano is, actually, quite surprisingly tall.

During the week I'd slept in my guest room, I had not thought to look at photographs of outer space, as Lozano had, but I did one time catch myself staring at a gallon of hand soap I'd bought some months earlier, stored below our kitchen sink, a preparation for the coming years with The Reason. I'd planned to refill the glass dispensers in the kitchen and bathrooms countless times, well into the future we spoke of often.

It was humiliating, crouching on the floor, staring at jugs of white vinegar and a liter of concentrated multi-surface cleaner, this faith in our future made physical, my plan to attend to the constant mess of our lives, the huge spaces of space ahead of us. We had never once discussed the possibility of ending this life we'd made together, and we had often planned our future using "in a few years" as an indefinite, yet definite period of time.

I went feral in a dozen ways as I moved out of that home. First, in trying to pack up every object that betrayed my belief in our future—all the soap, lentils in bulk, a whole pound of ground cinnamon—and giving this evidence away to friends; then I spent hours peeling every handwritten label off every jar I could find in the house, as it suddenly seemed very important that I leave no trace of having ever been there, and therefore no evidence of my absence. (Later, my friend Brenda laughed at this mad ritual, like the wartime practice of removing street signs to confuse the enemy.)

Hope is visible in the objects in our homes. Identities and plans rest dormant in a stack of books. The kitchen pantry reassures us of our future nourishment. A toolbox is the confidence that we can fix what will break. Little notes to self.

Little notes of self. The secret language of things we use to fold life into time, time into life.

But if I believed it was unfair that I had to shed all the hope I'd stored in those rooms, I needed only to remember how easy it had been to throw away the meaningless clutter at my father's house in Mississippi a few months prior. I undertook that purge while he was in the hospital, and though I was ostensibly clearing room for the domestic aides he would need now that he was bound to a wheelchair, it was also a selfish act—I could do almost nothing for him at his bedside other than witness his suffering, a task that seemed impossible to complete, while making the kitchen usable again was something that could be achieved over the course of an afternoon or two.

Dad had been stacking things on the counters for many years, church programs, newspaper clippings, coupons, junk mail, receipts, free calendars from every liberal nonprofit, hundreds of semiread magazines, and endless notes to self in his all-caps hand, often the same note—PLUMBER—by the stove—PLUMBER—by the sink—CALL PLUMBER—set neatly by his placemat at the breakfast table. The accumulation bewildered me, but later I understood that it was just the way a man who had been living alone for two decades had been marking the passage of time: the church services attended, the weekly and monthly magazines, the papers he'd read or left unread. It wasn't clutter to him—it was measurement.

He had spent seven hours alone, in the part of the basement directly below his kitchen, when he was taken down by a stroke.

When he finally came home to see his kitchen stripped bare, he was alarmed.

Where are my things? he asked.

(Where is my life? he meant.)

What things? I asked, and it was in this way that I distorted his anguish.

When my grandmother still remembered who I was, but was beginning to forget, I asked her something I had always wanted to know: why had she and my grandfather, in the late 1960s and in the heart of the Deep South, divorced? There was no greater scandal or humiliation then than the end of a marriage; she'd been ostracized for it, had moved out of town, lived the rest of her life alone.

The divorce paperwork had stipulated that neither she nor my grandfather was permitted to entertain any suitors or remarry, else they'd lose all custody of the children. Each of them stood with an arrow aimed at the other, a mutual spite that couldn't have come from nowhere, and from the moment I learned of it I wanted to know what had caused it, what had made them choose a life of mandated solitude rather than another day beside the other.

We were together seven years, and then—she hesitated, as she looked up at the ceiling. *Well*—*we were married seven years, and then . . . well, then he died.*

(My grandfather lived another forty years, but I didn't correct her.)

Oh. What did he die of?

Well, she said. *It wasn't the war . . . It wasn't an accident. It must have been natural causes.*

Natural causes. He would have been about the age The Reason was when I last saw him, forty-something, and for many years I found my grandmother's total amnesia of this pivotal moment of her life to be humorous veering on tragic, but now it seems logical to simply forget painful memories that have nothing else to teach you.

A youth pastor told me once that when you repented for your sins, Jesus not only forgave you, he immediately forgot what you'd done, an absolution so complete it was wiped from history, and at one point toward the end of his life, the poet John Berryman was found lying face down in bed and hungover as he shouted, *These efforts are wasted! We are unregenerate!* Berryman was trying to find God then, but what he was finding instead was that it was very difficult for him to stop drinking.

A commitment to Christianity depends upon believing the story of that regeneration, but while God might eradicate the dark histories of his adherents with ease, it seems the rest of us need stronger and more dangerous things to forget our own: dementia, drugs, brain damage, fiction.

———

Everyone told me that everyone was breaking up or breaking down or breaking through those days—*these days, these days*, everyone said—something in the ether, it seemed, was pushing them all to the edges of whatever they were in. The pandemic was entering year three, and a friend's paranoid delusions returned, and there were miscarriages and estrangements, and nearly everyone's marriage was ablaze, and addicts were playing chicken with their addictions, and spouses were meeting strangers at the airport, then calling from foreign countries to say they're never coming home again, and the piano player couldn't play the piano, and the ex-wives became anti-vaxxers, and the neighbors kept calling the cops—*please, dear God, please, do something*—and all the while I kept writing down the facts, the sometimes barely believable facts of how much seemed to be changing, eroding, losing control, and I began to wonder if this has always been the reason I've written anything at all—to break reality down into a story, or to make a story into a reality. For a little while I wondered if there was measurably more chaos in late 2021, but it was much simpler than that. It's natural to pay attention to the unceasing troubles of others when, like passing by mirrored windows, you notice yourself in them.

Toward the end of Annie Baker's *Circle Mirror Transformation*, a character asks a question: *This is kind of weird—but do you ever wonder how many times your life is gonna end?*

The guy she's asking doesn't know how to answer her, doesn't even know what she's talking about, and very occasionally I wonder about those sorts of people, too, the ones whose lives never seem to end, just continue, then continue some more until they end completely. But I didn't seem to know anyone like that, at least not that year.

Even Manguso, the least-Californian Californian I know, suggested (then insisted) that I call her energy healer, and even though I didn't understand what an energy healer was, I called the energy healer. The energy healer said the word "rupture" so beautifully—*rupture*—that I understood immediately why someone would pay to listen to this woman say this word.

I no longer had enough information about who I was, I realized, while I was on the phone with the energy healer, a very kind woman in Massachusetts with a devoted following of people who do not exactly seem like the type to call an energy healer, but later I discovered I was still not the sort of person who wanted to call an energy healer, and apparently I was not even the sort of person who did not seem like the sort of person who would call an energy healer but still wanted to call this energy healer anyway, and as I got off the phone of what was essentially a very nice guided meditation, a secular prayer about the body led by someone who truly seemed to care and know something, I remembered the autumn after my stepsister died when she was thirty, and how I felt suddenly desperate to see a psychic, desperate for someone to tell me what would *happen*.

After I saw the psychic, however, the main feeling I had was the cessation of the impulse to see a psychic.

———

That winter everyone kept asking me, *What happened?* and I didn't know what to say.

I kept thinking of Marina Abramović and Ulay standing in the center of a gallery with their mouths locked together and their noses plugged shut, breathing in each other's carbon dioxide until they passed out.

And I thought of that young man I met in 2010 who had been floating on a surfboard off the coast of Samoa when the tsunami sirens sounded. He and the others had fifteen seconds to decide whether to paddle out to sea, past the coming wave's break, as one of them suggested, or to go inland and sprint from the beach as others believed to be wise, and the man who told me this story as we picked grapes in a vineyard in Gisborne several months later had paddled outward, beyond the tsunami's break, and he never saw the others again, and what happened to The Reason and me was something like that, too.

The more I tried to explain what had occurred, the more it felt like nothing had occurred. What happened? All those years together, you seemed so happy, then what? (*No children, no through-line,* a parent once told me, the implication being: no reason to stay.) Everything was just as it had always been, then nothing was as it had been. Everything was gone. But somehow—between normal and abnormal—nothing happened.

Nothing happened, I wanted to say. It was just the end of a family. It was just the end of a way of life. The Reason and I had entered those years suddenly with a pair of divorces and the kind of urgency I'd known only when I still believed in heaven and hell. What began as an intense friendship at a literary festival in Australia became him calling me to recite poems, calling just to say hello, calling just to listen to me breathe when I told him I didn't have time to talk. It was a proper courtship, Victorian in how certain he was about us despite a lack of consummation. The fact of my husband did not deter him, since I kept answering the phone. But after a few months of those calls I took the drug of his certainty about our future and found an adrenaline-addled, car-lifting strength. *Let's beat this thing for good*, he often said. Six years later, it ended just as suddenly, with the sale of our house, our deconstruction, my banishment.

I'm not banishing you, The Reason repeatedly explained before he suggested I simply stay in the guest room until we could sell the house. It was the kind of plan you'd suggest to someone you assumed had no self-respect, to live like a grounded teen for months until spring heated up the housing market, but what else can you call it but banishment when the man you loved and believed yourself loved by, the man with whom you'd bought a house in which you lived with his mother, whom you also loved and had probably spent more hours with than your own mother, what do you call it when that man emails you from the other room to explain that he met another woman last week and now it's over?

An email! A fucking email! my friend Tim shouted, laughing, more than a year later, still shocked by it. *People get fired with more dignity. Did he think you were his employee?*

It wasn't that he didn't love me, The Reason explained. It was that it had become clear to him that I didn't love him anymore. *This isn't what I want so much as it is what you want,* he told me, and when I said it wasn't what I wanted he simply said yes, it was.

Later it became clear—The Reason had the right to explain my feelings to me because he'd spent six years telling me what I felt and who I was, and had quite often been correct. Usually the version of myself he sold me on was more positive than the one I'd previously held. He believed me to be smarter than I thought I was, more capable, more powerful than I had previously thought myself. I began to believe him, and yet that belief brought with it a strict obedience to this person who had, it seemed, created me. Of course he had the right to tell me who I was, and what I should want or do. I had given him permission to do so.

I do everything quickly, The Reason had repeatedly said to me and to others, perhaps proud of himself, perhaps just aware of himself. *Everything.*

I tried to go see his mother for the last time. I texted to ask if I could come over. She said please come over. I let myself into her apartment that adjoined ours as I had hundreds of times for dinner and teas and afternoons spent quilting and drinking wine. She tried to make us a cup of tea, but didn't seem able to move, just stood there with watery eyes— she hadn't seen it coming either—because it was certain this would be the last time we would see each other as family, in the home we'd shared. I paced the room, unable to find anywhere to sit, unable to find the exit, unable not to cry, busily moving around like a bird that flew in mistakenly; then

I ran down the stairs and away without quite managing to say goodbye.

Awake well past my bedtime as a child, I often tried to reason through how I could ever know if Jesus was truly in my heart.

Had I adequately and genuinely invited Jesus into my heart? How could I be certain? And how could I prove it to anyone if not to myself? How could I approach death—just an accident or illness away—with such a loose grip on my salvation? It troubled me. I prayed while looking over my shoulder. I prayed as if it was an act of espionage, dire and delicate.

All the pastors said you had to have faith, that it was always a matter of faith—faith that Jesus was in my heart, faith that I deserved grace, faith that I was on the right path—but how could I be sure I was truly perceiving my faith and not my hubris that I had faith? Did you have to have faith in your faith? And where would such faith-buttressed-faith come from, and did you have to pray for that, too, and anyway how could you even be sure you had prayed to the Real God and not some False God that grew like mold in your human mind? How could you be so certain your prayers had reached God and not been intercepted by the Devil? How did you know the Devil wasn't the one answering your prayers, parroting the voice of the Lord?

Part of what terrified me about the Bible was that the

people who killed Jesus did not know they were killing Jesus, the real and actual Jesus, and if Jesus came back to earth, it seemed inevitable we would kill him again, or perhaps we already had. It was a huge misunderstanding—the whole crucifixion thing—a gratuitous miscommunication that had created the entire worldview to which I was deeply devoted.

Yet isn't there a bit of smug indifference in the way Jesus hangs there on the cross? It's as if he knows precisely what is going on and has already risen above it, as if he is thinking *You people think you're killing me, but I am actually an eternal deity that cannot exactly experience a mortal death and will be worshipped infinitely into the future.* Nobody killed Jesus, but we were forgiven for it anyway.

Do you ever think maybe he was right? Max asked, several seasons later, a bright spring evening over white wine. I knew immediately he was asking me about The Reason, that Max had never seen me this happy, how better off I was now that more than a year had passed. Perhaps The Reason, somehow, had known about this improved version of me. Perhaps by telling me I didn't love him anymore he was doing me some twisted kindness.

But it becomes true the minute you say it, I told him. *"You don't love me anymore" means I disallow you from loving me.*

A little cloud passed in Max's eyes, maybe imagining his own wife saying as much to him or him to her. Or maybe he was just hoping for more grace on my part, a pardon for his friend.

The question only reminded me of the cruelest part of the

whole thing, how vividly mundane those days had seemed, how The Reason had looked, at most, a little concerned for me, yet still above it all. I didn't love him anymore, but he had already forgiven me for it.

I sat on the kitchen floor as The Reason theorized that the reason I had stopped loving him and the reason we hadn't had as much sex as he would have liked was that I was, most likely, just a lesbian.

This was news to me, but like everything he told me about myself, I tended to believe he was right, that he knew me better than I knew myself, as he seemed to know everyone better than they knew themselves. *I'm a lesbian?* My two most significant relationships had been with men, and sometimes I wondered if the shorter ones with women were enough to even call myself queer.

I sat on the floor beside the oven, sensing my reflection in the dark glass. The idea that I didn't know I was a lesbian seemed patently false, yet The Reason was so often right. Sometimes—thinking he must be wrong this time—I would correct or challenge something he said only to discover later that he had been right. Sometimes I would correct him and offer proof that I was right and he was wrong, but he was so accustomed to being right that he tended to become fragile and angry when it was suggested or proven that he had been wrong, and even then he would find a way to argue that in fact he was still right, in a sense, right as long as you passed through a side door and ignored all peripheral vision and instead went straight to his rightness. The Reason was and likely still is rhetorically unstoppable, and his students often began to imitate his style or ideas or ways of speech as if they'd been filled with a parasite that replicated The Reason's beliefs inside of them. I'd seen it over and over and over. He amassed a little cult around himself without seeming to even try; so compelling were his diatribes and pronouncements that it was difficult to resist the conclusions he made about how to live, how to write, how to think; and even as a stubborn woman of thirty-six, distrustful of authority, prone to rebel, even I considered the possibility that I may have missed something all these years, and maybe he was right—I could have been, all along, beyond my comprehension, a lesbian.

On a freeway in Los Angeles at dusk that December, I admitted the worst to JV: *I loved being in that cult.*

I cried in JV's car as he drove me to the second or third holiday party of the night, and it felt both strange and sacred to be carried around by my friends like that for weeks—*So your life has been emptied out: let's fill it back up with parties. It's the most wonderful time of the year.*

I held sunken eye contact, and I had no appetite and no alcohol tolerance, and my blood pressure was so low I could have fainted at any moment, like a pallid background female in a Victorian novel, and still my friends insisted on more holiday parties, said I had to get out. *Happy Holidays*, I repeated in a strained monotone. My clothes hung from my shoulders as if I were a child who'd pillaged my closet pretending to be a woman somewhat like me. But there were more cheerful times, too, like the night I pulled a beautiful new friend into my winter coat and made out with her, perhaps to test The Reason's theory, perhaps to try to catch Covid so I'd be excused from all the holiday parties, but I didn't catch Covid, and kissing her felt the same as kissing a woman had always felt—like kissing a person, insignificantly different from kissing a man. I started conversations by asking people about what they'd lost lately, drew strangers out about dead dogs and broken love and foreclosures of all sorts. I told them the hardest part was losing his mother overnight; then I slipped away to cry in strangers' bedrooms or to leave without saying goodbye. Before that winter I hadn't spent much time in California, and though I'd gone there to live with my friend Haroula, it also seemed that there was no better place for someone to tread water after being kicked out of a semi-cult than hopeless, hopeful California.

When I wrote to Manguso to tell her of my trouble, she told me her spouse of fourteen years had recently left her for another woman after a long affair. *Everyone's breaking up these days*, everyone kept saying, and though the ambient heartbreak had been no comfort, it was unpleasantly pleasant to learn of an ending more extreme than mine. It's a cyclical pain and a shared one.

When I arrived at her home, she asked me a few questions like an intake nurse, then showed me to the backyard. *See that wall?* she asked. Part of the white wall around her garden was covered in dents and gashes; I did see it. I had some idea of what she'd been doing.

She'd bought a pallet of bricks and had been hurling them, she said, breaking them into chunks and shards. Her son had joined in, too, the two of them expelling the rage from their bodies.

We took turns throwing them that morning, then she watched me, newer to the wreckage, commenting on my form, handing me brick after brick.

Aim low, she advised. On the other side of the wall, kindergartners were taking their recess.

Manguso had been the only one to say it—*I'm not going to tell you that it will all be OK.*

Everyone had been telling her that all year when what she needed was for them to recognize that everything was absolutely not OK, not even a little OK, that she felt she might actually die from what was happening within her. I knew what she meant. I kept picturing a hand emerging from my mouth and reaching down to choke me—not a suicide but a circumstance, natural causes.

I, too, was tired of people telling me there were good things in my future, and though I distantly understood they were right, I didn't care about that future goodness, as I was living so intensely in the present that the future had no meaning. It did not exist. It did not exist at all. It was supposed to be a good thing—living in the present moment—but how grim it was to find that it had never been easier to live in the now once the now felt like a town that had been tornadoed away, not even wreckage, just a sky without a horizon, nothing to orient around, no sense of north.

Even now, long past the initial shock, my old moods have taken on an inscrutable sheen, as if they happened to someone else, or as if they were just some odd fiction I wrote one afternoon in a bad mood.

It's been a hard year, Brenda said, smoking in her living room, one of the very best places on earth, that heaven on East Eleventh. I told her I couldn't remember the last winter that at least half my friends haven't looked back at the year with dismissive rage. When was the last New Year's that every incoming text at midnight didn't read, *To hell with 2016, 17, 18, 19, 2020 . . . !*

While Brenda was out of town for a few days, I stayed at her place in Manhattan, getting to know the keys and the leaking radiators and the various kinds of jam in the fridge. There's no intimacy between friends quite like living in their apartment without them. I tend to pretend I *am* the absent friend: smoking if they smoke, reading whatever's on the nightstand. During the week at Brenda's I urgently needed to be someone else, ten days post-email, the ghost of The Reason at my back, the unforeseen future before me. I walked to and from East Eleventh with Brenda's shrugging gait, ate at the places she would eat, took my coffee like she takes it.

Manhattan is and has always been the best place I've known to cry in plain sight, so I did a good deal of that, too.

Much has been written on the subject of crying in Manhattan, as writers tend to cry in public, and writers tend to congregate in New York City, and anyway, you could make the argument that half if not all published writing is a form of crying in public.

I cried openly on the subway, on many sidewalks, at a cafe in Park Slope with Eric, then a chic Midtown restaurant with Jin, and after warning the woman sitting beside me, I cried all the way through an opera—*Eurydice*, a classic doomed romance hinging on ill communication—and without warning anyone I cried discreetly in a coffee shop, and later a bookstore, a park, a museum, a pharmacy, then I stopped crying for long enough for Jackson to take a photo of me smiling beneath autumn leaves, and though I tried to repress it, I could not help but weep while crouching to pet a stranger's dog.

Around Thanksgiving I made out with a friend of a friend like teen virgins, but then we started talking about the people we'd lost, and we both started crying and parted ways with too much emotion—*I feel like I'm never going to see you again*, he said—and how the stakes had gotten so high so quickly made no sense at all. I never saw him again. Everyone, absolutely everyone, seemed to be freaking out. Even the copy on a jar of peanut butter tried to offer advice—*Separation is natural*—and as I was trying to write an email an error message appeared: *Oops! Something went wrong!* My internet connection was unstable, the computer said, and I was unstable, I knew, and I had to click OK only to, twenty seconds later, confront the same message. *Oops! Something went wrong!* OK, I told the computer. *OK OK OK.*

The Reason wrote to say he missed me. I told him dead people can't miss anything. I was exaggerating, sure, but nothing, it seemed, wasn't an exaggeration.

When I began to lose my faith in God at fifteen, I lost my appetite, completely, for years, eating only because it seemed I should eat and never because my body had asked for it. A passage in Corinthians had been the compass for what to do with the spiritual liability of my flesh—*the body is a temple . . . ye are not your own*—and once I had slipped loose of the belief that the Bible was the word of God, I had no law, no rubric for what to do with myself. I had believed a body was nothing but an altar to the Lord, not my own, not anyone's own, just something I was borrowing as the physical site of my devotion. I packed rigidly balanced sack lunches as a preteen and worried about artery plaque, and preached to a boy at school I'd heard was stealing his mom's cigarettes. *For ye are bought at a price*, Paul told us, *therefore glorify God in your body and in your spirit, which are God's.*

Without God, what was a body? Just a place to wait.

Parables confused me with their debatable messages, so I latched on to the more specific directives with passion. After reading Leviticus I announced I would no longer eat pork, and though my mother tried to explain that we, as Methodists in the twentieth century, didn't have to do that, I told her she could do whatever she wanted but I was going to follow the Bible, the actual word of our actual Lord.

Whether false idols might be lurking in my imagination (I had a troubling fondness for a certain Lilith Fair singer), or whether I had unquestionably and successfully invited Jesus into my heart, or whether it was OK or not OK to be "prodigal"—all of these issues were unclear, but not eating bacon was something I could accomplish and check off the list the same way "Thou shalt not kill" and "Thou shalt not commit adultery" had been so easily checked off.

I know exactly when I stopped loving the Lilith Fair singer—her fourth album felt like an aesthetic betrayal—but I've never been able to clearly see the moment or moments I stopped believing in Christianity as the one true religion of the world. The scene is always out of focus, just offstage, somewhere in between reading Hindu and Buddhist texts or fielding the eye rolls of girls I tried to preach away from premarital sex and drinking, or maybe it had more to do with falling deadly in love with a sixteen-year-old androgyne beauty who was, unapologetically, an atheist. We were together for two years during which I was still terrified of premarital sex, thinking constantly of hell as he held me. He told me he was willing to wait forever (which he did).

The Amish had Rumspringa, but Methodists had no rite for testing a secular life. I stopped praying, stopped witnessing to kids at school, stopped protecting my temple from poisons like lust and cigarettes at the Waffle House. I expected that I would, like all biblical characters before me, be taught a lesson and return to the fold, but in the meantime there was no discernible God, and without a God—without a reason for life or death—what good was a body? I asked this question. I had no answer.

Hunger was the closest ancillary I had to the rapture I'd felt when I went to the altar as a kid with open palms at weekend retreats, or the nights in silent prayer when I felt—or swore I could feel or needed to believe I could feel—the hand of God resting on my chest, or the mornings in church when I knew every word of the sermon was a message just for me, just at the right moment, divinely sent. Hunger was a pure devotion to the nonmaterial, and its hollow suffering felt like an act of faith, a denial of the world as I waited for heaven.

But there's no drug, no love, no bodily sensation or metaphor that comes close to fully believing that the creator of the universe had transformed his son into a human being who came to earth to work miracles only to be executed for *my* sake, for *everyone's* sake, and though this truth had been obscured for some reason, it had been revealed to me, and now I was regenerate, and now I had to tell everyone else this very Good News. I felt like I was standing on a cliff overlooking a placid, boundless ocean, and I knew that there was perfect order and harmony all over the universe, that I would one day be reunited with everything and anyone I would ever lose in this life and everything I never had in this life, and we would glow in heaven, and the world would be over, and the evil would suffer in Hell, and the virtuous would not even remember them. I would be lying if I said I didn't miss that metaphysical certainty—all the riddles solved, everything in its right place.

Hunger—no, the absence of hunger that comes after hunger—is the closest replication I've found for the cold clarity of faith. But even so, it is synthetic; eventually you must eat.

My teenage body quickly melted away. I was taken to doctors, psychologists, nutritionists, therapists, and forced to weigh in daily at the school infirmary where I was a boarding student. I knew all those adults likely saw another delusional anorexic—silly thing, little girlish terror—but I didn't (I couldn't) mention my religious confusion or grief. To say you didn't believe in God felt like taboo of the highest order.

I didn't have the self-awareness to know I was practicing asceticism, a denying of the flesh perhaps in order not to lose Him. No one would have taken me seriously anyway, and I knew it. What could some teen girl know about God? I was a little younger than the corpse of Joan of Arc.

Over espresso with Sasha on one of those suddenly warm, spring days in New York, he told me addiction is now described as a bio-psycho-social disorder (that is, a disorder of everything caused by anything), because the more we study it, the less certain we are about it—what are the possible reasons and roots of self-destruction? And what are the roots beneath those roots? And beneath those again? Many who have chosen to go hungry will recall how addictive it is.

A great indignant thrill came when my bloodwork was

deemed acceptable for a teenage girl. (I did eat, a little—vegetables for the vitamins so I didn't fall ill.) The therapists couldn't locate any particular phobias or body dysmorphia in our sessions. My period went away but I didn't tell anyone, though when I tried to sign up for the blood drive senior year, my blood pressure was too low to find a pulse—*Honey, I'm not sure you're alive.* For a while I was put on Prozac, then I stopped taking it. The nurses tsk-tsked as the scale numbers descended, but a wild blond a year older than me gave me rocks to hold in my pockets.

Fuck them for trying to control you, she said. She hid her own medications under her tongue and spit them out.

The wild blond was impossibly beautiful and cool and unhinged in a way that she seemed to control, somehow. I could never figure out why she was on my side, but perhaps she was just on the side of not being controlled—she with the Beastie Boys poster in her dorm room and the occasional joint she smoked fearlessly out her window. Sometimes she would pull over on a dark road in the middle of the night and dance in her convertible's headlights—she met at least one boyfriend this way—and it's a miracle she graduated, that she survived at all. God must have been looking out for her, I sometimes thought, devotion be damned.

I didn't even tell her about my recently passed devotion; it was shameful the way a middle-school perm or an embarrassing past fandom is shameful, and ignoring it was easier than seeing those years as foundational, something to which I would always be reacting. The campus reverend hosted a Bible study at his apartment some weeknights. I went a few times, never speaking, just showing up and waiting, as if everything could be reversed if I put myself within reaching distance of God.

After The Reason sent that email, my appetite left, completely, for the first time in more than twenty years, and it was only then I could viscerally remember what faith had felt like—this bright feeling in the nerves, a sense of being porous and airy. Reality was clear. Death was an illusion. I stood in our kitchen where I had cooked and eaten a thousand meals, and was unable to eat a piece of toast, as its texture and smell were an affront, somehow, a noxious torture where there had once been comfort.

Even the pleasure of toast is gone, I texted to Tron. *Even toast.*

Don't blame toast! Tron wrote back, but I was prepared to blame toast. I was prepared to blame anything or anyone, prepared to see the world as packed with villains.

Tron's six-year relationship imploded the same month as mine, so we had been commiserating on our suddenly empty days, on storage units, on the petty conflicts obscuring the real conflicts. A sense of picking up midconversation has always defined our friendship; I'd been listening to Tron's music for a year before we met, an album I had been unaware contained a line from my first novel they'd repurposed as a lyric, so we'd been speaking to each other for some time before we ever spoke, and it's continued like that, this irregular conversation.

In a park on Thanksgiving Day, Tron taught me how to push myself around on a skateboard as a trio of their friends cheered me on. They were all being so kind. I was out of place—a grown woman wearing the wrong shoes, as thrilled as a toddler or a dog would be thrilled to simply roll in a straight line until the inertia ran out. I spent most of that afternoon watching the four of them—quite young and spry and pliable—ollie off concrete stairs and tumble off their boards, taking the missteps as they came, accepting the pain and accidents built into the art of gliding and balancing. Pavement is a skateboarder's ally and foe; she resists gravity, then yields to it—resist and yield, resist and yield—always searching for grace in the transitions.

A skateboard was one of the few things I permitted myself to almost unapologetically want as a kid. (I asked for it several Christmases, reluctant but hopeful, though it never came.) But wanting something or asking for something was terrifying, as I feared that human wants were necessarily in contradiction to the will of God, a force that could be ignored only for so long until his wrath came down.

The real reason I was never permitted a skateboard was that I was a girl, and this was simply not a hobby my father would permit his daughter to pursue. This was also the reason the middle-school bandleader told me I could not play the snare drum, since *boys play the drums.* He suggested the flute instead—*it will fit in your purse*—but I told him I didn't carry a purse and quit band. (And, lo, the rage I felt the Sunday when the bandleader visited my church as a part of a small orchestra, proudly pounding a timpani.)

When I told my father I wanted a skateboard, he said I would break my whole body, that I was simply not up to the task. It is true I broke both a leg and an arm and got stitches in my scalp before I was ten, yet the threat of injury—physical or otherwise—may be requisite to anything that's worth doing, and maybe that's what's so compelling to me about skateboarders: the jollity they have about pain, and the faith they have in their ability to transcend it.

Starving had that in it, too—a feeling of being connected to something larger and mysterious, something outside the body, something divine that might, at any moment, reach down and crush me.

For years I grew gaunt, and when a friend or a parent or a teacher would point this out, I ignored it—it simply was not a problem. I felt fine. I didn't care what I looked like, and I assured everyone again and again about how fine I felt. I would sometimes eat something large and indulgent to prove how I didn't care, how it must be the fault of a fast metabolism.

Sometimes I wondered if the point of all that cold and somber pain might one day be revealed to me, that God would appear again and convert those years of hunger and beyond-hunger into wisdom itself. I was waiting then and I am perhaps still waiting now for something divine to happen, to be punished or rewarded for denying the flesh for so long.

At the end of our first winter together The Reason came to me with pity in his eyes. He told me I'd put on a little weight and he was concerned; he didn't want this to begin a pattern. I said nothing in response as he suggested a new schedule for when and what I should eat, how I should cut out certain foods and increase my daily exercise.

I listened to everything he had to say, then I locked myself in the bathroom to weep for half an hour, and later I went for a long walk that ended at the zoo, where I kept weeping as I held eye contact with a gorilla. It's true that in colder months I might gain a few pounds, a winter softening that never required new clothes and certainly didn't bother me. But it had apparently bothered him.

No thirty-year-old woman, I knew, needed anyone's unsolicited opinion on her weight, and while I thought it was absurd for him to expect my form to remain static, I didn't know how to square that knowledge with my belief that The Reason was more practical and impartial than I was, so I searched for an interpretation of the situation that would make my reaction a matter of oversensitivity and hysteria, something that could render The Reason's reasoning unimpeachable. Perhaps I had gained more than I realized, I thought, but when I weighed myself the addition was minuscule. Well then the scale had to be wrong, even though my clothes all fit just fine. Still—The Reason had to be right. My reaction, my weeping, was so female and embarrassing. Crying about a few pounds? Grow up. Better to be detached about this, to accept this minor fact, to acknowledge that he was right, that I should lose this weight before it stayed.

The fact that I had chosen to cry in the bathroom and go for a long walk alone had apparently surprised The Reason so much that he almost apologized, but I assured him it was fine and that he was right. Within weeks I'd lost it all, and when I wore a skirt and top to a party that showed the smallest triangle of midriff, he pointed out I wouldn't have been able to wear such a thing if I hadn't lost those few pounds. It was then I must have first and most deeply conceded to the idea that The Reason had the power to tell me, at all times, in all ways, who I was.

Every day there were new customer service representatives to call to unwind our lives. Utilities, insurances, the phone company, the bank, the vet, airlines. Contact information to update. Account beneficiaries to alter. The Reason's name had burrowed into everything, like glitter in shag carpet—*in the event of my death, in case of emergency, if found please return to.*

A call with a T-Mobile representative was more dramatic than expected. I was living with my friend Sara then since I was effectively broke until our house sold. I sat at her kitchen table as I explained to the delicate voice on the line that my relationship had ended, that a second phone number was no longer necessary, that I needed to terminate that additional line.

A sharp inhale from customer service. *Of course it's hard for me to do this,* she said, *canceling a line, but I will do it.*

It sounded as if she were giving a lethal injection to a suffering pet, but it was just a phone line, a number, a nothing. I smiled and rolled my eyes at Sara, who smiled back—and dear God, the smile of Sara, what a holy thing—but then I stopped smiling in order to meet this customer service representative in her funereal feeling.

Sometimes you have to just take it out back and put it out of its misery, I said.

There was a long silence on the line, then a hesitant and determined, *Yes.*

It's OK, I said, trying to comfort her as she killed those digits. *We're doing this together. We'll get through it.* Sara raised her eyebrows and muffled a laugh, but I was deadpan, committed to the bit.

Moments later, when the customer service representative told me it was done, that the number was gone, that it was all over—did I hear a little jolt in her throat?—she asked if there was anything else she could do for me, anything at all, and I said no, there was nothing; then we solemnly wished each other well.

During the first year of lockdowns the three of us watched episodes of a *Sherlock Holmes* series from the 1980s. Each hour was a repetition of the last—impossible mystery, mysterious chase, surprising resolution—a soothing completion when so much else felt undone and pending. But in the second season, Watson was replaced by an actor who looked a lot like the real Watson, but just unlike enough that I was unnerved. Who was this false Watson? What right did he have?

I had never realized how integral Watson was to the world of Sherlock Holmes. While Holmes has an acuity and bravery that is nearly deific and impossible to entirely identify with, Watson is our human conduit, a reliable but markedly less remarkable man through whom we can connect to the great detective, and the entrance of this substitute Watson removed me from the story, an irritation that I first used as a joke—biting my thumb at him to entertain The Reason and his mother, CB—but eventually my irritation became sincere. I lost interest. Where was the original Watson, my Watson, the actual Watson? Season two was all wrong, and why, exactly, why was everyone carrying on as if our Watson hadn't been killed off and eerily replaced?

When I left my husband Peter, he told me that I no longer looked like the person he knew, that I was someone else now. I thought then it might be something of a comfort—the false wife standing there, similar to but ultimately unlike the original wife. Now I am unsure whether comfort is the right word for it, now that I've seen The Reason's face peeled off The Reason, something cut out of him and therefore something cut out of me.

The first winter I knew CB, after dinner with some friends at her apartment, the fact of her knife collection came up and she got them all out to show us. There was a nice pocketknife or two or three, but also a hunting knife, a cleaver, a very sharp paring knife, a second type of hunting knife, a

Japanese chef's knife, a hatchet, a knife that was historic in some way I can't remember; then there was the machete she kept in the closet. *Aren't they wonderful?* she asked, beaming at the knives—that elegant, basic tool of survival, cooking, art, protection. I had never seen so much awe on someone in their seventies—and I felt moved by her ability to be joyful after the hell I knew she'd been through. It must be one of the most difficult tools to keep sharp over time, awe, a faith in finding the beauty of anything.

The Reason and I accumulated several good knives in our home, too, and on one of those sleepless nights after being fired, I found myself standing naked in the kitchen, looking at all our knives. I had no purpose in doing this. I didn't plan on stabbing myself or him, and I wasn't going to cook anything, and I wasn't going to hide them or take them with me. I just got them all out and looked at them. I tested them for sharpness. They all needed to be sharpened. The house was dark. Nothing was moving. I was alone. The knives always needed to be sharpened, I thought, but hadn't we just taken them to the sharpener? We had wrapped them in brown paper and given them to the professionals, asked them to transform our knives into something more dangerous, more accurate.

Il vaut mieux couper que déchirer (It is better to cut than to tear) was how a woman I don't know told my friend Paul, over the phone, that she was leaving him, suddenly, after their seven years together. It had been decades since that cut, and he now has a wonderful wife and children, gratifying work, boundless enthusiasm, but I could still see it, deep in his eyes, a finely accentuated scar.

Leaving our knives, I found the crowbar on my bookshelf that had been left behind by our home's previous owner. I held it, too, there in the dark, for no understandable reason other than the illogic of insomnia had asked me to catalog every implement of destruction available in the house, anything I might hold up in defense of myself, my right to continue to exist, which seemed to be under threat from some unseen assailant. Weeks later in New York I took long, aimless walks, paying special attention to the points from which a person, hypothetically, might jump. It wasn't that life was meaningless without the family and the home I'd loved for so long, but rather that this suddenly new life was too meaningful, saddled with so much meaning there was hardly any room to live.

It's not a will to live that's keeping me alive, I typed back to Jim when he asked if I was OK. *That sounds like something you would write*, he said. *That's because it is something I wrote*, I replied.

It felt clear that I should die, that I should be killed, taken out, really, by some freak accident—an air conditioner falling from a window, or a bus driver meeting a sudden seizure, or the gulp of a sinkhole. Ideation of a violent, sudden death or suicide began when I was a kid, imagining my own body crucified as a way to empathize with the Lord, or imagining burning in hell as motivation to do right, but over the years it morphed into an anxious tick that appeared whenever thinking overwhelmed me.

Before that day in Manhattan, eyeing the heights, I felt sure suicide was something I would never have the intention or capacity to carry out, but how could I be so sure of myself now that so much I had been sure of had gone? Yet even then I wasn't wondering if I was going to commit the act but whether it was going to happen to me, as if it were something wholly beyond my control. Yet it's possible that no one can know how seriously they hold an impulse toward suicide until it's too late to know anything, so I called Sasha and asked him to walk with me.

If you want to go away for a while, he said, *walk into a hospital and say that one word.* He'd done it before, gone away like that. I knew I wasn't there, but I needed the mirror of a friend to know it. We walked on for a while, then stopped to say hello to his fiancé at her office, glorious view from that eleventh-floor window—*and that, for instance, would work—* then we wandered through Greenwich Village and passed, perhaps by accident, the apartment he'd lived in with his first wife, the mother of his sons, decades prior. She and Sasha had divorced long ago, but their boys had kept them together in the way that children will, and eventually they had turned the dial of knowing each other back to a new start. Recently, however, she had died. Cancer. Rather sudden.

Now there's no one who knows how happy we were up there, he said, looking up at the same fire escape that would have saved their lives if it ever needed to. In her last days she didn't want to see her first husband or almost anyone else. Standing there on the street, Sasha trembled.

I didn't get to say goodbye to my friend, he said, and I hadn't either, and I cried for both of us, cried for the unnumbered time that week, cried as if someone had slapped it out of me, convulsing on the sidewalk as New Yorkers passed by like they'll pass by anything.

Was it necessary? Was this the only way? Was it better to cut than to tear? Better for what, for whom? These weren't the right questions to ask, but I kept asking them until it became clear that the only thing you can do if you wake up in a life you don't recognize is to get up, wash your face, proceed into the day as if you know exactly where you are.

When she asks if I'm OK, I tell Haroula I'm not depressed, it's just Christmas, my ex's birthday, his fake little baby body in mangers all over the place. This holiday used to mean something immaculate—the divine descending into the human, the first of many miracles—but now it's just a slow, cold day, one of the darkest all winter. That year was the first I'd ever spent Christmas alone, and how odd to find it more comforting that way. I gifted myself a pack of cigarettes that I took two months to smoke. I went to a movie. It was all much easier than I'd expected.

I'd fallen out of touch with her for the last year or so, then Emma called to come out, that year's Christ, reborn as a trans woman. It was Emma's first Christmas being out to her and her wife's Catholic families, so we compared notes on our odd holidays. What had been lost, what had been gained? Who had said the right thing and who hadn't? How were we making it through?

Emma told me about a man in her family so angry that

a trans woman was now his relative that he spent the entire Christmas party standing in the front yard, choosing to sulk alone rather than breathe the same air as his trans relation. It was funny to us, absurd even, the image of this man out there in the cold, his sheer stupidity preventing him from having a holiday, but I knew I was also, sometimes, the angry man in my own front yard, not wanting to be in a house with myself, a person I did not yet know.

In moments of weakness and depletion, I look for the unwavering order and certitude that used to accompany my religious extremism, but all I find, instead, are friends who read tarot, and charming little coincidences, and the infinitely flexible explanations of astrology that everyone now seems obliged to know. What I want instead are blazing miracles. I want crystal clear visions, a burning bush, the voice of a goddamn god.

When I was a kid I was riding my bike with my friend Luke at the far end of our neighborhood, on a dead end that pitched downward into a steep driveway. Luke went down first, expertly turning so as not to crash off the embankment, but when I followed I flew over my handlebars, cut my head open on some bricks, and rolled into a ditch—a moment of shock, then the feeling of warm blood trickling through my hair.

Luke panicked and fled to find help, but just after he'd gone a man in a white shirt and white pants jumped over a nearby fence, picked me up, asked where I lived, and began to run me home.

I'd never been the kind of kid who wanted to play the damsel in distress in playground games, but now I could see the appeal, how powerful it felt when my trouble summoned a bespoke hero. The man in white could have been in his twenties, thirties, maybe, but in a neighborhood where everyone knew everyone, it felt unusual that I'd never seen him before, not on the sidewalks, not at the picnics, nowhere. Unruly blond hair, deep-set eyes, totally calm. Was he someone's dad?

He deposited me in a chair in my parents' kitchen, and I can't recall now whether his white shirt was covered in my blood or conspicuously clean, but either way I felt that he—whose name we never caught and whose face I never saw again—was some kind of miracle, an angel or a sign to me that I was protected and virtuous and divinely beloved. I would have bled out on the concrete, I thought, I would have died right there at the end of Oak Grove if it weren't for my faith, the little thread from which I was always hanging.

I wished we had gotten his name, as he certainly had one, but my mother was more concerned with her daughter's head wound than noting where to send a thank-you card, and later I told kids at school about my miracle, this strong and seemingly unexplainable man in white who jumped a fence to save me, an angel, surely, as there was no other explanation.

Order out of chaos. Divinity in happenstance. Meaning, meaning, meaning; everywhere I turned as a child, there was meaning salving and saving me, telling me I was correct, telling me that I was saved and powerful and protected eternally, so long as I kept believing.

On the eleventh day of the eleventh month I was supposed to get a haircut at the eleventh hour, but a call came that morning saying the hairdresser had to cancel all her appointments, and at eleven past the eleventh hour, I opened an email from The Reason, *Please Read—urgent.*

The Reason refused to use a laptop, so I did most of his paperwork, e-signing PDFs and filling out forms, my willful participation in the long lineage of women licking stamps for their geniuses, his at-will secretary, which is all to say that I expected *Please Read—urgent* to bring some sort of time-sensitive document until I read it: *I am speaking in this letter about the dissolution of our relationship as partners.* But he wasn't speaking, he was avoiding the sound of his voice, the look on my face, and it wasn't even a letter, it was an email. He would have typed it on his phone.

I walked loose legged down one flight of stairs where he stood there like a man holding a knife over a chicken's slit neck. The ink was still bright on a love note he'd left for me before taking a short trip, and I'd cooked all his favorites to celebrate his return.

What was that email? I asked, as chicken blood ran at his feet.

For weeks after this, it seemed everything had an eleven in it, or happened at 11:11, and on the one hand I knew that the number eleven had nothing in particular to do with anything, and that I was simply noticing every eleven as it arrived, as numbers do, in daily life, but I could not completely shed the feeling that every eleven now meant something or that they should mean something, even though these numbers meant nothing upon nothing, and I knew that, too.

And when I went to sell a portion of my books to lighten the load for wherever I was going, JR tallied them all and came up with a price, turned the calculator to me—

How's that for a cosmic number?

333, the screen read, and immediately I thought of the three I was losing—The Reason, CB, our dog—the three of them standing there, three threes saying goodbye to me as I was saying goodbye to these books. I shook my head at JR. *Wow. How about that?*

Shedding books is something I hate doing, as a shelf is a kind of diary, a map of a past and potential self. The Reason had often read books aloud to me and I to him while soaking in the bath. We'd read *The Wind in the Willows*, and I'd read him Lydia Davis, and he read me *Dubliners*, and we read each other our own work, sometimes, and every year we all three listened to Dylan Thomas's *A Christmas Story* on Christmas, and when I'd gone through my books, picking which to leave behind and which I couldn't part with, I opened the ones he'd given me and ripped out the dedication page and kept it and gave the rest away—destroying evidence on the one hand but keeping track of it on the other, keeping the proof that we had been in love, that we'd had a real life. Later that day, driving my friend Jenny's truck around a corner I'd walked past countless times before, I noticed, somehow for the first time, a 333 painted in huge letters on a wall.

Weeks later a scientist friend told me that in times of high novelty—say, when we travel or start college or are casually banished from our lives—memories are formed with greater precision and depth. As he explained this to me, I remembered how I've tended to reread parts of W. G. Sebald's *Rings of Saturn* when my life seems to be falling apart—the morning after my father's massive stroke, for instance, or the first days I was marooned in Los Angeles—as that book has had a way of making every fleeting memory and fact I've ever known feel both worthy of holding on to and impossible to even try to keep.

It is probably a mistake to think of coincidences as metaphors happening in real time, or as messages in disguise, but I know I have an appetite for finding these hidden clues, and for weeks no matter where I went in New York or Los Angeles I kept running into old friends and acquaintances who had just crossed my mind—Pavli at a bar, Tommy at a concert, Kyp in a courtyard, Deenah at a new friend's house, Adron at the potluck—and all these people piled up so high it began to seem absurd, as if some kind of memo had been sent out, a continuous flash mob of what felt like everyone I'd ever known.

Months later, walking into a new lover's home, I noticed the apartment number—1111—and months after that, killing time before coffee with a friend, I wandered into a clothing store and came across a hideous little T-shirt screen printed with a paragraph explaining that 11 is an angel's number and seeing 11s often means an angel is trying to contact you, and fifteen minutes later, I paid for our fancy coffees and found the total, with tip, to be $11.11.

No one cares about anyone else's coincidences, I announced, in a bad mood at a good dinner party. A beautiful, young drummer with big sincere eyes shrugged and shared hers anyway, which I cannot remember (like other people's dreams are rarely remembered), but everyone agreed her coincidence was, indeed, remarkable. Then we all forgot it.

I went to see Geoff in Venice Beach, thinking he would say something no one else would say about all this, something wry and dislocating.

It's a relief that Geoff—an Englishman—tends to wince when a conversation veers into the personal, like a bowling lane bumper to prevent too much emotion. I told him I didn't have any contact with The Reason anymore, and he told me a story about a Serbian woman he was with for many years but left abruptly when he met his wife. The Serbian woman refused to speak to him ever again, a promise she's kept for decades now. Every few years he thinks of her, and sends an email; nothing ever comes back. He knows she's still alive—or someone told him she was—but they're both getting on in years now and he wonders . . .

He didn't finish the sentence, so I finished it for him: *You wonder if you'll talk again before you die?*

Yeah, he admitted, squinting at the ocean.

I thought of her out there, holding out in Serbia, impervious, and I wasn't sure if she was an ideal or a warning.

There's an outline of a heart just below my left elbow, a tattoo I took as a ritual of joining The Reason's family, half of which is dead. The outline was taken from one of the eight solid black hearts The Reason had tattooed on his body after his brother and father died a few years apart, a heart traced off their gravestones, a heart CB had taken from an old sewing pattern. I told The Reason when he died I would fill it in like the ones that would still be on his corpse. I felt so sure I had many years, decades, before that came.

When I met Topo in Juarez, I told him that if I began weeping during the tattoo it wouldn't be from the pain and not to stop, as I feel very little when I get tattooed, but I didn't cry during our session, just for a little while outside the studio, sitting in the sun for a moment knowing The Reason, or at least The Reason that I knew, was dead and never coming back. While the ink was being cut into my arm I listened to music, talked with Topo, and laughed in a way you can laugh only when doing something drastic—then again maybe tattoos are less drastic than they seem, as getting one makes the concept of permanence seem like a physical thing, just a matter of a little pain, a little ink, a little time.

What I miss about church are the rituals—the candles and robes and processions, the predictable order of the services—and as a kid I envied the lush extras that Catholics and Episcopalians had in their incense and motions of the cross and confessions and kneeling.

I used to keep the communion cracker in my mouth and let it soften slowly on the way back to the pew where I finally swallowed it, drawing out the pleasure: the salty flesh of God's son ripped and killed for me, ripped and killed again each Sunday at the altar.

But after you're not saved anymore, what are you? Spent?

My friend Francis couldn't play the piano, couldn't or simply wouldn't, wouldn't or just wasn't, and whatever the reason was I didn't like the sound of it, so we made a bargain: if he could not play for himself, I would call him every morning and he would play the piano for me. It would be my job to listen and his job to play, a mutual task, as I needed obligations, and he needed to leave his mind and return to his hands.

As I proposed this plan, I admitted that it was slightly ridiculous and perhaps overly intimate for a friendship as distant as ours, *But I don't care how it sounds*, I told him, as the only things it seemed I could do lately were things I'd never done before. I was walking down a busy street in the dark in Los Angeles as I proposed this. I can't remember where I was coming from or going. I wasn't sure if I was asking him for help or offering my own.

My childhood biblical interpretations meant I should never ask for anything, help included. I was afraid of the line between basic needs and cravings, between living and lust. If

I asked others for help too often, it may seem to God I didn't trust Him to offer help when I actually needed it, and such quarreling with life could only bring on His wrath; I was so sure of it.

Each of my calls with Francis began the same way—brief hellos, how are you feeling, then one of us would ask the other whether they were ready, and the reply was always the same. We were always ready.

I had pictured myself writing as Francis played scales or practiced songs, but for the first few days his hands hardly remembered the keys, and I had nothing to work on, no thoughts worth keeping, hardly any thoughts at all. He played slowly, sometimes with a metronome, shards of chords or songs in parts for no more than a few minutes, but after a week he began, as if by some miracle, to sing, and I muted myself and folded onto the floor to cry, not for him and not for myself and not for anything other than the fact that any pattern can be broken, that there is no end of patterns breaking down. Weeks went by and months went by, and I called him from different cities, different rooms, and over time he could play a little longer, a little freer, songs he knew by heart and songs he was still trying to write. It was as easy as it was unusual, this distant company, this regular puncturing of our tendencies toward solitude and shut doors.

I admire and envy the way a musician can practice in comparison to the way that writing is practiced. The fact that a *practice space* could be shared, or that some musicians sometimes gather to improvise, is plainly alien to me—that an act of creativity could be so interpersonal.

I spent a few days in Topanga, in the home of a friend of a friend, a man I'd never met whose marriage was ending. The house was hallmarked by the coming divorce—the wife's closet vacant, the family portraits somehow pained, the bathroom cabinets ransacked of everything but expired medicines and nearly empty shampoo bottles—but I felt at ease in the unease, and very close to the strangers who had lived there.

Weeks later the real estate agent sent the photographs of our house for the listing. The Reason, who was still living there, had made no effort to make the house seem not what it was—a place from which someone had fled. One of the photographs showed a room I had just repainted still haphazard and deconstructed. What had been my office was empty of everything except a chair-less desk and an empty dresser. The bookshelves I had cleared in the living room were filled, oddly, with rolls of paper towels—yet I *knew* there was space in the utility closet for paper towels, though The Reason had never seemed to remember this, and repeatedly asked me, with each passing roll, if we had more paper towels.

I'd assumed The Reason would tidy things, rearrange them, make the house seem inhabited by anything other than ghosts. I felt sorry for the people who would come across these images and try to imagine their lives happening in those spectral rooms, but the prospective buyers would probably feel sorrier for whatever had happened to the people who were leaving them behind.

Nothing in those photographs belonged to me, but I felt exposed by them. They all reminded me of the absent wife's walk-in closet in Topanga, empty of everything but rejected wire hangers and an unpaired sock. After weeks of thinking of it, I raised the nerve to ask the agent to retake the photos, to stage the rooms to suggest people might live there.

But then I thought of the mornings when Francis fumbled a note or fell short of his falsetto and how he used to shyly apologize, and how over time he stopped saying he was sorry and simply continued, allowing the errors to live.

On the surface, the choice to appear completely naked in a short film seems extreme, or at least requiring some courage, or madness, or a fluency in nudity, but when I did so in a field in Tlayacapan with three people I barely knew, I felt neither mad nor courageous nor a natural. I felt (though it felt surreal to feel) absolutely fine.

The only other time I'd been naked in front of a camera had been fifteen years prior, on a lark, a story I'd never told anyone. At the time I lived in New Orleans, and I lived on cash gigs, and I came across an ad for an artist whose studio was just around the corner from where I was temporarily living on a work trade, alone in a huge, empty mansion in the French Quarter that was in some legal limbo. The artist who photographed me was slow-moving and slight and had a rare eye disorder that made his vision blind spotted and soft, but he kept making his paintings and photos anyway.

I felt his work was tacky, not that my opinion mattered. He used his models' naked bodies as canvases, obscured them completely with his hyper-detailed paintings of landscapes and animals; he then photographed the result, the body of the model almost totally hidden in the paint. I wasn't entirely sure why I felt interested in being a part of that process—this bizarre intimacy and objectification and vanishing—but it seemed a worthwhile trade for a few hundred dollars.

To get the gig I had to first strip down for test shots, but after I'd gotten dressed again the artist told me, flatly, that there simply wasn't enough of me, that I was too un-fleshy for his task. I did not, to my surprise, take it personally. I'd mostly recovered my appetite by this time, but my body had not recovered from the years of deprivation, and the moment the artist denied me the job, I felt this message had been the real reason I had answered his ad: I was trying to echolocate—*Am I here? Where am I?*—trying to put out some kind of signal and receive something back, something to repair this estrangement, the sense I had of subletting my body from its true resident.

For months after leaving Chicago, bathing or undressing was confusing, as I'd lost so much weight so quickly, my own hands didn't recognize my body. I eventually found ways to echolocate by swimming in the ocean or having sex or taking psychedelics, so when I was asked if I would play the naked, masked hierophant in a short film retelling of the Persephone myth, I almost immediately said yes.

The next day I was naked save for a whole-head mask that practically blinded me, running through a hedge maze. Everyone got confused trying to puzzle their way out at the end, and even though I'd been navigating the maze in the dark, I remembered every turn; I was the one who guided us out.

My grandmother, as a girl, had been caught playing with her mother's rouge—*I want to be seen*, she explained with the pilfered lipstick on her mouth—and as punishment her father took her downtown to the Piggly Wiggly where he worked, lifted her onto the counter, and announced, *This is Martha. She wants to be seen*. This may have been the last time she ever asked for anyone to look at her.

She and her sister were outfitted identically as children, in dresses handsewn by their mother. In the unpublished memoir I read after she died, my grandmother explains it was her father's idea for his daughters to be dressed the same so that no one would think their parents were "partial" to one over the other.

When I think of Mother's making us two of the same garment, she ends the paragraph, *I feel inferior*.

Spring 2013 was cicada season upstate, and I'd never seen such a thing—as all their singing, fucking, and dying transformed the fields and woods into a strange bacchanal. Peter had taken me on that trip, and as I looked at him then (before he became my husband, then my ex-husband), I knew that I was the cicada in that relationship—a bit more (a bit too?)

intense, more prone to howling. We were new to nonmonogamy that year; we were trying it out like ice skaters testing the thickness of a frozen lake. I took a photograph of an insect corpse and captioned it, *Cicada season: have sex and die.*

My stepsister, MG, was ill back in Mississippi, but I didn't yet know how bad it was. I had been told she was acting strangely. The last two times I'd been in town she had not shown up to either dinner we were supposed to share. I didn't understand what was happening, but later it would become clear: she needed a liver transplant but couldn't stop drinking.

It was the same summer my brother was getting married, and the morning after his wedding in South Carolina as I made the long drive back to Mississippi to see my stepsister in the hospital, the call came.

When we were kids, MG was my idea of a creative genius, a powerful mind, a person who was entirely alive; she contradicted nearly everything about what a Southern girl was supposed to be. She was brash, opinionated, loud, passionate. The only way she conformed was in her exceptional beauty, musical talent, and willingness to perform.

A few weeks before MG died, I met The Bad Idea at a party in New York, and when I got back to the city after the wedding-then-funeral, I started sleeping with The Bad Idea, though he was exactly as advertised. I had not felt much about him when we met, but after MG's death he'd become a portal to the past, back when I'd been drinking gin at a crowded party, not thinking constantly of cicadas and MG and oblivion.

The first reason The Bad Idea was a bad idea was that I knew I couldn't trust him, and the second reason was that he quite obviously did not respect me, and yet in grief I was writing bad fiction and passing the time with other bad people and doing other bad things, and in comparison to all that The Bad Idea wasn't *so* bad, ultimately, as he was intelligent company and he made me laugh and forget my troubles, and under it all I suspected he was at least good-natured in his badness, as if it were some kind of genetic disorder, something totally outside his control.

It was difficult not to notice how women he had wronged were liable to show up and shout at him when we went out together, or else send him menacing texts about having seen him here or there with a new girl. I kept sleeping with him anyway. I didn't care that he was a bad idea, as I, too, was a bad idea who could not stop thinking of all the other bad ideas out there. It seemed to me that having a family was a bad idea and loving anyone was a bad idea because dying was a bad idea, yet—oddly—not dying was also a bad idea, and having sex as much as reasonably possible felt like a way to die and not die, a way to lie down and never get up again.

After he'd read a short story I'd written he told me that my fiction proved that I was something of a scoundrel, which was fine with him because so was he. Two scoundrels, I thought, just two scoundrels doing scoundrelly things.

My grief over MG morphed into a hunger rage. Peter did not understand, so I broke up with Peter, then spent as many nights and afternoons as possible that autumn with other people's bodies, these temporarily wonderful but absolutely disintegrating things, and I felt so much anger toward organs—spleens and kidneys and hearts and livers—and no amount of seeing and being seen naked by people, no amount of grabbing someone's waist, or holding their skull close to mine, no amount of sensation or being held or being thrown around could set me right with the living world.

By the winter, repentant and tired, I tried to analyze the grief sex. Ecstasy had a way of both contextualizing and warping loss. What I wanted from fucking seemed discontinuous from what I wanted from my life, and I could hide from the impossible thing I desired by seeking something achievable and small—another hour or so sunk into sensation. In December I surrendered myself at Peter's apartment as if I were his lost luggage.

What I really wanted was for MG to be alive and grow older with me. I wanted for her to get past the dark years she'd been in and return to who we had been as children when she'd taught me what it meant to be fully affected by art, music, singing, love. It had never occurred to me that she could end at thirty, and it seemed not just wrong but unreal, and I wanted a total redemption, to time travel, to escape all facts and reason, but I would have to settle, instead, for a period of sexual heedlessness that I hoped might be some kind of portal, some kind of redemption. In the end that time didn't really do much other than pass the time.

Vulnerability does have the power to adjust pain, but all I'd been doing in sleeping around was participating in a theater of vulnerability, not the real thing.

A month after leaving Chicago, I called up The Bad Idea

after many years of radio silence and went home with him, an attempt to return to a time in which I was also trying to return to another time. The Bad Idea was still chronically dishonest and a lot of fun, same as he ever was, just eight years older.

There are at least two fallacies in grief sex. The first is that it turns a private truth into a shared truth—feelings in unison, in union—and the second is the belief that such a shared space could be continuous postcoital, that an evening's pleasure could correct the loss that pervades the day. Maybe the first fallacy is true, at least slightly, or at least symbolically, but the latter never is. When a lover leaves the bed, the lover stays in bed.

Socrates spoke of the Ancient Greek myth that cicadas were the reincarnated souls of those who worshipped the muses in ecstatic states so intense that they forgot to eat or sleep: those who died dancing, died fucking, died singing, and were rewarded for their madness by coming back to briefly relive a short life of ecstasy, then die again before it became too complicated. I took this myth so seriously. I had my photograph of a cicada turned into a tattoo on my left arm. I still don't know what I thought this myth could teach me, but I was determined to learn it, no matter what it might cost.

On a hill above one of the cabins I lived in during that drifting winter after leaving my home, there was some kind of yoga school or healing center, and occasionally I saw people wandering up the dirt road toward it. I never went up there and never asked anyone what it was, but once or twice a week I could hear a chorus of wailing—primal scream therapy, I guessed—and their noise comingled with all the birdsong and pig grunts and that one goat with the oddly human cry, all of them howling what they could not say.

Why did I so immediately smile those afternoons in that rain of human screaming? Was it heartening to hear strangers expelling their traumas, or was this simply a nervous reflex, an impulse toward balance when pain meets a witness?

In shock in Chicago, I had cried for so long it turned into a kind of scream, an unexpected and embarrassing howl. The Reason had looked at me with the shrink-wrapped concern I'd seen him give to the students he met with through an iPad screen.

I hated to be so unhinged in his presence, as I didn't want his pity and I knew I had none of his respect, and I wanted to refuse, even, his blithe tolerance, a face immobilized by indifference, and yet it was funny—I had to admit it was funny—how I kept apologizing for my mood, how I couldn't stop crying and shaking and spitting up pure bile, then catching my breath to apologize for it. I was sorry to be such a mess, sorry to make all this noise, sorry to be unmanageable, that female training kicking in, as always.

When I asked if he was upset, The Reason said he'd mourned the end of our relationship slowly, in private, for months and months. He'd gone through his own piecemeal mourning right in front of me, without a word, smuggled out like a house removed brick by brick. If I had really been paying attention to him, he explained, if I had really loved him, then I would have known what he was feeling. I would have known how dire the situation was. How had I not read his mind?

This should not be shocking, he said to a woman quite clearly in shock.

A blur of days later, I was sitting in my office, idle, too abject to be abject anymore, listening to The Reason play an endless funeral hymn on his shakuhachi when my phone rang. It was one of the women who had been dressing and feeding and bathing my half-paralyzed father back in Mississippi. She was calling to quit, she said, as she simply couldn't take it anymore, couldn't take my father's anger, couldn't take his insults, his shouting, couldn't take any of it another day, though she loved him, she reassured me, she loved my father and wanted him to be better but he wasn't better—he was giving her hypertension and insomnia, and he had crept in as the sole subject of her therapy sessions, and she was crying every day at work.

A grown woman, she said, *I'm a grown woman and I can't be treated this way.*

Months later, a passage in Simone Weil reminded me of how my father had treated the caretaker and of how many parents have treated their children: *To be able to hurt others with impunity—for instance to pass our anger on to an inferior who is obliged to be silent—is to spare ourselves from an expenditure of energy, an expenditure which the other person will have to make.*

My siblings and I were running out of people to hire in that small town, but I didn't ask her to give my father another chance. I told her I understood, that she absolutely shouldn't be treated this way. I wished her well.

Before his stroke my father had tamed the angry person whom I had spent my childhood fearing; he'd gone to therapy, read the books, gone on spiritual retreats, and though he hadn't exactly apologized, his changing was a kind of apology. He hadn't been the absolute worst, anyway, not as bad as I knew other dads to be. We had all been afraid of him, and our fear had created obedience, and our obedience led to an orderly home. He'd read to us regularly and at length, and took us to museums and the theater, and even though there was a kind of rigidity to our cultural literacy—mandatory participation, and quizzes on what we'd learned—at least we had been cared for in this way.

The stroke had peeled all of that recovery away and revealed the erratic wrath he'd once held, an echo of his own father's anger, which was most likely an echo of *his* father's anger, and so on and so on. At least this time the source of my father's rage was obvious—this massive and nonnegotiable brain damage, the sudden removal of his every independence. He'd been a notably spry sixty-seven-year-old—occasionally mistaken for my brother, swimming daily, drinking never, graying only in recent years. His stroke, indifferent to all this, had sent him into a wheelchair. I was mad about it, too.

The night I got the call about Dad, I was having dinner in New York with Sara and Sean. The Reason was with us, too, though I can't remember, now, him being there at all—I can't see his face or remember how he reacted to the news. What I do remember is standing in Sean's living room, crying like a hurt child as he held me. The Reason did not care much for my father and was often protective of me when it came to him—resentful of the angry environment of my childhood, encouraging me to distance myself from him, to feel less about him, to see myself as owing him nothing.

Around Christmas my father called and asked me how The Reason was doing, and I said he was fine, that he was the same as always. Dad hadn't gotten a Christmas card from CB. Did I know why? *No idea*, I lied. He asked why I was in Los Angeles instead of spending the holidays with them. I did not answer honestly, but a few days later I came clean about my breakup with The Reason. I even told him about The Reason's rage, though I stopped short of telling my father I'd been well-trained to accommodate such behavior.

Maybe The Reason had mourned our relationship through his anger—the slammed doors or thrown objects, or the time he called me a crazy, sexist autocrat for wanting to leave a light on in the stairwell for a female friend who was staying in our guest room, or that one time he punched a wall and broke part of his hand and could not reasonably go to the hospital given the risk of bringing the pandemic home to his asthmatic mother. He had to let his busted hand mend itself, which it did, crookedly, and painfully, though he rarely complained. I had checked my phone during a film he had wanted me to watch—that was why he'd punched the wall.

It was no secret that The Reason had been even more violent in the past, that he had brutally beaten up other men all through his young adulthood, that an ex-girlfriend had told their mutual friends he'd hit her (he denied this), and that a few months before we met, he'd been taken into a police station, his shirt covered in a stranger's blood. While biking in Chicago he had shouted at a careless driver who made the mistake of getting out of his car to confront The Reason. A fight ensued. The driver was outmatched. The cops were called. By the time they arrived, the other man had fled. The Reason was taken in, but he charmed the cops and was let go without a charge, and he told me all this without pride or shame, as if summarizing one of his own fictions.

I knew all of this well before I agreed to enter his life. Sometimes he seemed so placid, so unflappable, and other times there seemed to be a feral animal thrashing just under the skin. When we met he often spent several hours in daily meditation in order, in part, to quell the anger that had so long been a part of his life. At times it did seem to be working; at other times, less so.

Several years passed before the effects of walking on eggshells around him showed up in a piece of short fiction I wrote. A young woman, a student of the narrator, writes a poem—*if you're raised with an angry man in your house, | there will always be an angry man in your house. | you will find him even when he is not there. | and if one day you find that there is | no angry man in your house—| well, you will go find one and invite him in!*

There was a tacit belief between us that the fictional poem had nothing to do with him, or with our home, or with me, or with any particular angry men I knew, and when those particular lines became a Tumblr, then Twitter, then Instagram, then TikTok meme—posted and reposted by young women and attributed to me as if they were a direct quote—he would roll his eyes, and I would roll mine.

Ha ha, we said, *yet again someone has confused the voice of a fictional character for an authorial statement of belief. Ha ha ha.*

The suggestion that an angry man might be found *even when he is not there* was my trapdoor, the soft suggestion that perhaps I was just inventing things, seeing an angry man where there was simply The Reason's reasonable frustration with me. I abetted his anger; I protected it. I understood his rage as something nonnegotiable about his masculinity, something I tolerated with the awareness that his latent capacity for violence could protect me. When an intruder broke into the apartment he'd shared with his first wife and her daughter, he sprang into action immediately, fearlessly chasing the man with a knife until he fled. And when I told The Reason about a sexual assault that had happened years before we met, he was enraged and told me he wanted to find this man and destroy him, and though I didn't want him to do so, I was darkly pleased by knowing that he could.

During arguments he would sometimes punctuate his frustration with me by slapping himself in the face, twice or three times in succession. The first few times I was appalled and asked him not to do it again, but within a year I'd started to mimic this self-flagellation, feeling oddly pious as I did so. Appalled, he asked me to stop. I told him I would stop if he stopped and neither of us stopped. Then, during a particularly ugly argument not yet two years in, he slapped himself, and instead of doing the same I told him he should just hit me and get it over with, that it was obvious he wanted to. It was a cruel thing to say and I'd never been so cruel to him. His face broke as if tears were coming but no tears came. He denied it, and said such an accusation was impossibly hurtful, that he would never forget it, but I remained silent and felt sure I was right about him. If he could tell me about what I was thinking, it had just occurred to me I could do the same.

The last time there had been such anger in my home I had been a child and my father, though he loved his children, hit us all in order to make himself heard. I knew what I was facing in The Reason, I told myself, even if he did not, even if he had the ability to turn his hands against himself in order to stop their impulse toward his woman. In some ways, when I slapped myself, I was doing so on his behalf. In other ways, it was a religious gesture, an act of supplication to him, to us, an attempt to force myself to repent my sins with my whole body.

The Reason also had a habit, for a while, of *playfully* (his word) slapping my ass when I wasn't expecting it, though I told him, indignant, that I did not like it, that it hurt, that I did not think it was fun. But he was only being, The Reason reasoned, *playful.*

At least once I reflexively burst into tears, though I am unsure now if that was the last time he did it or not. I told him it recalled the feeling of running down a hallway with my hands behind my back as my father came after me with one of his irregular punishments for whatever childish wrong I'd done. But I was putting limits on his affection, he said. This was a loving, intimate, playful gesture, and I was trying to paint him as a villain, as a kind of man he obviously was not—the hurt in his eyes! How dare I accuse him of such a thing! Another observation from Weil: *What is base and what is superficial are on the same level.* "*His love is violent but base*": *a possible sentence.* "*His love is deep but base*": *an impossible one.* But I did feel violently and powerfully loved by him, able to provoke huge, disproportionate emotions without warning. Weil might call this superficial; I'm not sure what I call it.

I wonder what he looked like leaving the police station with not even a tick on his record, whether they gave him a different shirt to wear or whether he'd spent the entire visit with the cops wearing the blood of that stranger. After that encounter, he had to have surgery on his right hand; he had broken some of his own bones in the blows he landed on that man's body and skull.

The Reason often suffered intense migraines, and I'd never known what to do when he was stuck in bed with a pillow over his face. Sometimes he wanted me there, sometimes he did not. Weil wrote of her own endless headaches, admitting they often came with the *intense longing to make another human being suffer by hitting him in exactly the same part of his forehead. Analogous desires—very frequent in human beings.*

I came back to visit Haroula in the spring, and one day we were discussing why someone she loved kept trying to take care of an ex who had been emotionally manipulative and abusive. She couldn't understand it, was worried for her friend, and as she peeled an orange for us, I asked her a question I thought had an obvious answer:

Haven't you ever tried to love or take care of someone despite being given ample reason that they cannot or do not want to receive your love or care? A faith it could go differently. An amnesia of how it's gone.

Haroula thought for a moment, very still, then handed me a half orb of orange. *No,* she said. *Why would I do that?*

Ah. Yes. A good question, I thought, a better question than mine.

In line at the airport, I was angry at Seneca.

On Chelsea's advice I was reading *On the Shortness of Life*, though I couldn't find a hard copy in time for a flight, so it was a PDF on my phone, a format that felt distinctly un-stoic, though no less stoic than being angry with a two-thousand-year-old ghost. I used to see Chelsea around Brooklyn when we both lived there years ago, and I always felt there was something oracular about her work—direct and true and unflinching—but also her appearance: long, black hair that draped like a hood or a veil.

Apparently Seneca believed widows should be permitted to mourn their husbands for ten months maximum, a precept meant to counteract *the stubbornness of female grief*, but what had any ancient man ever really known about any female anything? How could any of them have been so sure that it wasn't all an act, that she wasn't a bit pleased, that it wasn't just relief that led a widow to dwell in her black? What says *leave me alone* better than a veil?

Still, sure, I could see how there might be value in putting time limits—though not prohibitions—on mourning:

For to be afflicted with endless sorrow at the loss of someone very dear is foolish self-indulgence, and to feel none is inhuman callousness. The best compromise between love and good sense is both to feel longing and to conquer it.

Fine. OK. Fuck you, Seneca, but yes, it seemed to me he wasn't wrong, though I did not want, in that moment, for him to be right.

While waiting for an agent to sort out some problem with my ticket, I remembered a Latin phrase I'd first read in Nietzsche: *amor fati*—a love of one's fate, the stoic imperative to not only accept the life you lead but to love each turn of it, no matter how ugly or painful. The woman who was trying to check me into my flight seemed increasingly dismayed by her computer screen. She had to bring a colleague over to help out—never a good sign—but I tried to love even this, the minor discomfort of travel purgatory.

Taped above Lozano's desk in Mexico was a handwritten note: *Lo que sucede, conviene.* Roughly: *What happens, suits.* I glanced at it daily for weeks, reciting the line in Spanish and in English, and though I can't say I accepted it in either language at the time, I knew it would be better if I did find a way to release myself from my stubborn "female" grief.

Earlier that winter as I was eating latkes in Los Angeles with a witch I'd just met at Sammy's house, she told me she knew I was a lucky person, that my life was charmed, that everything I needed tended to arrive on time. I was feeling distinctly unlucky at the moment except for the fact that I was eating fried potatoes and drinking wine in a living room full of beautiful women (*All of Sammy's friends look like sexy cats*, the witch said, *I never know what to wear*), and really, what more could anyone want from an evening? Maybe the witch was right.

Fifteen years prior when I'd been interviewing a psychic Druid for an essay, he told me almost the same thing when I mentioned the insecurity I felt about how I'd ever support myself since I seemed only to enjoy doing things that had very little financial value. He seemed almost angry as he explained my anxiety was useless because money would come to me when I needed it.

Me in particular or—

Yes, you in particular! he said.

One of the things I liked about the Druid was how annoying he seemed to find his own abilities, and how it seemed to shock him that no one was as psychic as he, but on the point of my future financial luck, I was skeptical. He had also predicted, with glad certainty, the date of his death, but he lived past it. Perhaps it was a metaphor? A symbolic death? But I didn't want a metaphorical livelihood—I wanted a real one. I wanted (I still want) health insurance. And yet for the majority of my adulthood, jobs or windfalls *have* arrived as soon as the bank balance gets precarious, and each time this happens I cannot help but think of the Druid, his sneering smile, his shoulders draped in pretty snakes.

Amor fati should be easier for the fortunate to accept, and I have been so, yet isn't it also true that a person will encounter a finite amount of good fortune in life? And maybe I'm coming to the end of mine. Maybe it is a good time to learn to love my fate.

As a kid I'd felt nervously inadequate to make the most of what I thought to be the good luck in having been born into a churchgoing family in a theoretically Christian region of a nominally Christian country. It was my responsibility—*my privilege!*—to save everyone who had not been thusly chosen, to find them and persuade them, one by one, to live the life I was living, to join me in this nervous, burdened, unstoppable task of convincing the rest of the unsaved world of the metaphysical certainty of accepting Jesus as our one true Lord and Savior.

Anxiety bristles under many an evangelist. Weil:

Each time that we say "Thy will be done" we should have in mind all possible misfortunes added together.

Yet it also felt distinctly un-pious to really accept my station in life as something I deserved—I was no Calvinist—and so I could never relax into it, not even after seeking the advice of my youth pastor, who insisted there was no point in struggling against God's unexplainable grace, but I did feel guilty, or rather I felt embarrassed to be myself and not one of the millions of kids my age who hadn't been born straight into this, this path toward eternal salvation.

Decades later, bitter for the opposite reason, I was complaining to Brenda—distinctly not amor-ing my fati— bemoaning all the languages or skills I could have learned if I hadn't spent a dozen hours each week at the church or studying the Bible or going to retreats, and of course she shook her head, wouldn't let me get away with it. *Obviously you wouldn't be the person you are now if it hadn't been for those years*—and I tried to interrupt but she wouldn't let me—*and you wouldn't be the writer you are, you wouldn't have the perspective you have, the concerns you have, the anything.* [deep cigarette drag] *You can't argue with it, can't argue with your life.*

Friendship has a way of re-revealing the things you know in such a way that you can't help but accept them. Books can be such a friend, too—shedding light on a feeling the reader has already felt in order for her to see it more clearly, or differently.

Still waiting at the airline counter, it occurred to me that I ought to have *amor fati* tattooed somewhere conspicuous on my body so I'm forced to remember it, to account for it, to love what I do not naturally love, to go willingly and joyfully into whatever unmovable things occur: deaths, betrayals, homes burned down, canceled flights, books that refuse to be written, late trains, crashed cars, illnesses, and dead ends of every sort. A woman nearby—burdened with luggage and children—could not believe the news that their flight had been canceled. She did not love it. I could not blame her. I turned my focus back to my agent, whose eyes had taken on a glassy, cartoonish worry.

Naturally, one should be skeptical of what a professional mystic tells you about your fate or the innate predicament of your life, given the role manipulation can play in jobs that truck in the immaterial—religion, psychology, academia. I had not paid the witch nor the Druid for services of divination; each of them offered their confidence in my future for free. Yet believing in one's innate luck felt distinctly American in the very worst way. Did the Druid and the witch employ this optimism as a strategy? Not necessarily to get or keep a votary, but to spread some ambient hope around?

Weeks after latkes with the witch, an acquaintance, Molly, emailed to ask me what I thought of optimism. She had also reached the end of a long relationship, and was moving states away in our new country of uncertainty. I typed a reply in total confusion, unsure of what I thought until I read what I'd written. Maybe pessimism is the assumption that you know something you don't know in order to avoid disappointment, but if an optimist remains an optimist when the worst happens, then what is the cost of optimism?

I really don't know, I admitted to Molly in the end, *but it seems optimism is free and pessimism costs you something.*

When I'd written to Chelsea it had first been to let her know I was receiving much comfort from her book of essays and how reading them had reminded me that I had never checked in with her when our mutual friend died, Giancarlo, a cicada who had been persisting into his forties but succumbed to bad drugs in a Manhattan hotel room in April 2021. I'd been too hesitant to write to her as she'd been so close to him. In her words, everyone had expected her to *fall apart*. She hadn't done that, she wrote to me, hadn't fallen apart, and in fact it seems she may have come more firmly together.

I found myself very still, she wrote, *thinking about him fondly—sad, but not hysterical.*

It was as if her whole life of reading and study had trained her for that moment, and as I read those lines in the email I was stunned by the idea of being prepared to accept something so unacceptable, to not fall to the ground after the impact of the sucker punch, and again I saw Chelsea's black hair whip around a corner ten steps ahead of me.

Giancarlo's death had felt, for so many, totally unbelievable. I'd learned about it from Martina, my Italian editor and beloved friend in Rome, who emailed the word in all caps (*DIED*) as if to force herself to see it (*I can't stop crying*); and because so many writers loved Gian, the internet filled up with sentimental remembrances from otherwise aloof people, and I made it my job to read every word that everyone had to say about him, as if that was going to be some kind of tunnel back to his apartment in Rome, a meal he and his husband served me after a long journey, fragrant with olive oil, and Gian talking, nodding, smoking, and ready, always ready, for some long and unforeseen night to arrive. That day he was still a little dazed from a night out dancing with Martina and others, so he was going to take it easy, stay in, calm down, but again he saw the dawn.

I think if anyone could have told Gian he was going to go the way that he did, he wouldn't have been surprised, and perhaps that's a way to love one's fate, or maybe it's something darker, some kind of resignation, a quiet submission to be taken by the things you keep taking. *I hate drugs and his death made me despise them even more*, Chelsea wrote.

Pessimism might be an insurance policy against disappointment, and optimism a total buying into a different fantasy, but maybe a love of fate could be both and neither, I thought; then the agent at the airport confessed that the problem with my ticket was that it had been recategorized as first class for no understandable reason, and she couldn't find a way to change it back to the economy ticket I had purchased, hard as she tried.

The flight was long and international, and I felt quite chewed up by the last two months, and perhaps I never needed more than I needed then the ability to fully recline for a few hours. Certainly many people would have liked to have met that first-class fate, and now the idea of getting an *amor fati* tattoo seemed quite silly, me of all people. What did I know about the difficulty of fate? Nothing.

It was all so odd. In a coffee shop in the terminal a child knocked her plastic cup of yogurt off the table, and looking at it splattered across the floor she was quiet for a moment, then laughed.

A man was lying face down on the sidewalk. I walked past him, on an errand, within myself, then realized what I already knew—a man was lying face down on the sidewalk—so I returned to him and kneeled to ask if he needed help. He did not respond. Cars drove by. *Is there anything I can do for you?* I asked. *Someone to call, something, anything?* I spoke to him softly. I felt a strong sense of my own weakness.

Do you need help? I asked, which was of course an absurd question since he quite obviously did need help, but it seemed to me then that all I ever did anymore was ask strangers the most absurd questions.

The voice of 911 asked me if the man lying face down on the sidewalk had asked for help, or whether the man lying face down on the sidewalk was even in the position to consent to receive help, and though it was rather clear to me that despite his lack of consent this man would be better off if someone helped him—me, a medic, society in general—I had to admit that, no, the man lying face down on the sidewalk had still yet to say anything at all. I touched his shoulder, which felt even smaller than it looked there on the concrete, but he did not react. The Reason once told me how his father would wake him up in the morning by simply holding his bare foot until he opened his eyes, and I thought of that as I left my hand on this man's clothed shoulder. Here I am, his father, his stranger, awaiting his return. The man's feet—in blue socks and pink sandals—dangled halfway off the curb.

He may not want help, the voice of 911 said, *but if he doesn't want help, then tell him he will need to move somewhere else; otherwise people are going to keep calling 911 on him.* I told the voice of 911 that I wasn't so sure anyone else would call. No one was around. No one but cars.

Cities permit a certain amount of suffering in plain view as part of the etiquette of proximity, the privacies we afford each other in order to bear the burden of human density. I've walked past plenty of similarly prone people without a thought in the past, making some kind of calculation about the direness of their situation and the possibility that I could be an effective or welcome presence.

The Reason had felt ignored, he said, felt that he had been suffering for a year in front of me, and that I hadn't seemed to care. How sickening it was to hear this. I thought I had been caring for him in the ways I knew how—the thousand domestic actions, the long walks, simply being there—yet if he hadn't registered any of my actions as care, had my caring existed?

What else could I have done? I asked. *What did you want me to do?* We reached no specific conclusion on this point, but months later, suddenly awake in the witching hour, I remembered something he'd written in his memoir:

I love being sad, and in fact, it is a weakness of mine to allow myself to be sad for too long. Let someone who loves me try to comfort me, and I will just become sadder and sadder. It is better to rap me on the knuckles and walk away.

The voice of 911 asked, *Can you describe the man?*

I looked at the man lying face down on the sidewalk, now not entirely sure of their gender given the fact that their entire body, including most of their head, was covered in a blue sweat suit ill-suited for the heat.

I think he's a man, I said.

How old?

I can't see his face.

Twenty? Forty?

Closer to twenty, I guessed, as the voice of 911 kept doing what it did, a little paperwork to keep track of our emergencies.

Nearby two security guards got in their car and drove away. Someone must have been paying them to guard something apparently more valuable than this person.

I didn't want the voice of 911 to hear me crying. I didn't want to get too involved. If I stayed here long enough with this man lying face down on the sidewalk, I knew I would begin to love him in a way, but only as long as he didn't sit up and ask me to actually take him to where I lived and feed him and bathe him and love him for real. Then, naturally, I would have to run away.

The fire truck arrived. I began to leave, then hesitated.

Did they—could they—what would—was I?

No, the paramedic said—*you can go.*

Just before he sent the fire truck, the voice of 911 asked me to yell at the man lying face down on the sidewalk, to loudly get his attention, to tell him that if he didn't want help, he really needed to tell me now, tell me to tell them not to come. Was I trying to persuade him to accept help, or was I trying to give him a chance to refuse it, or was the voice of 911 trying to find one last way to not spend a resource on someone who wanted, in fact, to be left alone?

I'm not sure if someone who chooses to suffer or is attached to his pain can ever be soothed away from it, and maybe any effort to comfort such a person is actually an effort to change them and therefore not a comfort at all, but rather a bid to shape them into the person you want them to be. Persuasion or coercion may masquerade as a good influence or taking care, and it's possible that no one can be entirely sure which thing she's offering.

In *Swann's Way* there's an aunt who can only seem to care about the troubles and tragedies of strangers, and the less she knows someone who's suffering, the more she cares about that suffering, while those in her life get not an ounce of her sympathy. I've forgotten most of *Swann's Way*, but I've always remembered the aunt and the question innate in her character, how proximity has a way of bleeding into invisibility.

Before I knelt beside the man lying face down on the sidewalk, I first chose to do nothing, to walk by him, to not hear myself ask that question which I, myself, dread being asked—*What can I do for you?*

I tried to watch the flight attendant explain what to do in case of an emergency, but I had seen it too many times to see her. The oxygen masks, the exit rows, the seat cushion that can float. We know this. We all know this by now.

The pandemic was still drizzling on, so there were not many on that flight, just the people who really needed (or wanted or were being forced) to go somewhere, to leave somewhere, to flee. None of us were listening.

We know more about how to attempt to survive an aerial disaster than we know about meeting the end of love, the former being highly unlikely while the latter is close to certain.

Over lunch on a quiet street a married friend told me that her husband had asked her for a postnuptial agreement. It seemed humane, perhaps, but too late, as they were already getting separated, trying to read the informational brochure in the seat-back pocket as the plane was hurdling down in flames.

But she was not alone in being willing to prepare for imaginary disasters while refusing to imagine the commonplace ones.

Later I would describe that summer in rural Japan, unable to speak or understand almost anything, as feeling like I was reading a book for months. I had applied for the homestay with an essay saying that I, a child of the Bible Belt, wanted to live somewhere similarly but differently flush with religion. I must have had some naïve, American hope that going East for this reason would correct something or restore something in me, but all I found instead was that I spent all my time mute and confused, an outsider everywhere.

The rare memories of clarity stand out: there was the night I ate a particularly strong oshinko without wincing, prompting my awestruck host father to say, *You can be a Japanese*, or the day, later in the summer, apparently looking reedy, that I was led to the bathroom, placed on the scale, and told, *Not good*. I came home so accustomed to never speaking that I felt I was no longer fluent in English, just silence.

That fall another college freshman nicknamed me *"the skeleton,"* and I didn't care. That both strangers and people I knew would tell me what they thought of my body on a daily basis was unremarkable. A male teacher at my high school once informed me I'd lost enough weight, that I looked good now, but that I shouldn't lose any more, and one of my dorm mothers pinched my arm and grimaced as I walked back to my room from the showers in a towel, and MG once impulsively let the word *"disgusting"* slip, and men I didn't know of course had all kinds of phrases and signals, and it seemed to me that the only thing I could do was stand within my body like a stabbed stake, that I was my own, that no one was permitted to have an opinion I entertained or even heard.

In a harshly lit kitchen in my college dormitory, Sean and Wilhelmina, a pair of new friends who already seemed like old friends, fed me the first avocado I'd ever had. They—being from the East and West coasts—could not believe I'd never even seen one before, and had decided to correct this immediately, making a great vat of guacamole. I had looked down into it with suspicion, as I looked at all food in suspicion or confusion or disgust, but there had been something in the way that Sean said I should try it that had made it possible to do so, to eat in a way that was not difficult, to eat because someone was feeding me.

Eighteen years later I sat, exhausted and shaking, in his living room, as a bowl of chili he'd made for me grew cold on my lap. I could not yet eat, but Sean was there, and he had cooked for me for the thousandth time, and he could warm it again when I was ready.

The next day I walked a few neighborhoods over to see Wilhelmina and sit at a table with her children as she fed us all the same golden soup. I ate so much that I ached, and as I read stories to her son and daughter, they reminded me that there are things more important than adulthood, and in respect of their wisdom I waited until they had gone to bed to cry.

In Audubon Park as the sun was going down Sean told me about his choroideremia. He was eighteen and I was eighteen and all his choroideremia meant then was that he'd need a little help getting out of the park at dusk, and when we went to dark bars I'd have to guide him in and out by the shoulders. But the choroideremia was already closing in on his peripheral vision, and later it would send blind spots into the center, and eventually it would take everything and leave Sean blind. At eighteen the future seemed so far from us. It's much closer now.

They'll probably find a cure for it before it gets awful, he said, ever cheerful and nonchalant.

I've tried repeatedly to understand what he can't see— *Can you see this? How about this?*—but he's always told me it's livable, that he doesn't think about it, that he gets around just fine, that it's hard to describe, as if describing what it feels like to have ears on your head. Your ears are just there, *so* there, in fact, that it's hard to say, exactly, where they are.

One night I set a glass of wine before him, and he couldn't find it for a few seconds, and the next year it would take him twice as long to find the same glass. Now I take his hand and put things into it.

No one has cured choroideremia yet, but I know how to spell and say it now. There are clinical trials on a laser surgery and a gene therapy that comes in a single eye drop. Neither treatment could restore the sight he's lost, but it could slow or stop the erosion; I asked Sean when he'd start the trial, but he told me he hadn't yet signed up.

Why not?

He couldn't quite say why not. He kept putting it off, the phone calls, the paperwork, the train to DC. Maybe he would wait until more results were in. Maybe he would do it next week, next month. Maybe he wouldn't do it at all, and what if he did do it and it brought some more awful side effect, something less manageable than the creeping gray to which he's well accustomed?

The day I turned thirty-seven Sean cooked me breakfast and read my tarot and told me I was easy to love, and there are so few people who could ever say that to me in such a way that I could believe it.

I think sometimes of Sean taking the train down to DC, think of him walking into a large building, filling out paperwork, lying back in the optometrist chair, and I think of those experimental drops slipping over his eyes, sinking in, and how that will be the only and last and final thing he can do for his vision, a gate passed through, nothing left to do but wait. There are still, of course, other ways of seeing, of being seen. I think of guiding him out of a park at dusk when we were children and the future was somewhere else and we didn't know anyone who had yet vanished into it. I think of putting something into his hand.

———

A girl from church, someone's older sister, had crashed her car into the side of a concrete bridge, and after a long stay in the hospital she was back at church, standing in the room where donuts and coffee were served between Sunday school and the service.

I don't know how it happened, she said.

I felt her amnesia was powerful and peculiar. It seemed that she was taller than she had been before, and her face had taken on a seriousness I'd only ever seen in fathers.

The question arose of whether she'd done it on purpose, or done it in absence, if she *let go and let God*, as they said.

At ten I won third place in a poetry contest with eight rhyming lines about the inherent hopelessness of mortality and the necessity of Christian redemption. It was so obvious to me—How could you be Christian and not think of death all the time? Wasn't heaven inherently better than the earth? How could you not want to go there, and soon?

At seventeen I was driving north on the Natchez Trace when I lost control of my Chevy and flipped it forward off the side of an embankment. I hadn't been eating, and the road was wet and maybe it was overcast or maybe I was swerving to miss something or maybe my body just didn't want to be driving anymore, didn't want to be doing anything anymore. I couldn't remember.

All the impact was on the driver's side—the windshield smashed, the door crunched shut. I crawled out the broken window. I ran up the hill. On the side of the road, my hair fell out in clumps, and I smiled. Still alive. How absurd.

For a few months after the wreck, unharmed save for a

bloodied fist and a slight concussion, I felt not just that I was alive but *still* alive, a one-word reframing of life that carried the implication that if I was persisting, then there might have been something (not God) worth persisting for.

Family lore held that Aunt Mae, as a child with blond ringlets and a lisp, screwed up her courage on a Sunday to ask my grandfather, *But why don't God like hims debil?* Everyone laughed, and for years we kept laughing, but did anyone ever answer her? The impossible questions are the only questions. The existence of the devil revealed the limits of the God we believed to be limitless, and it was reasonable to wonder why. Children know this and adults pretend we don't remember.

Two years after Chicago, living a life I couldn't have imagined then, I was in La Pitaya, in Veracruz, sharing lunch with Isabel who, well into her eighties, smiled as she remembered protesting her first Catholic Communion. Standing at the altar, her parents behind her, the priest asked if she renounced Satan.

No, she said.

Her mother pinched her. The priest repeated himself. Still—*No*.

¡No lo conocía! she told me. "I didn't know him!" How could she renounce someone she didn't even know?

That's how good you were, I said. *Así de buena eras.*

I was having a drink in my brother's kitchen when he asked me if I knew that our father had hit our mother when we were kids. *I knew*, I told him. I may have even said, *of course I knew*, because of course I knew. My brother hadn't known, he told me, not until very recently. Last week.

My brother tends to be quite calm. He doesn't startle at loud noises, and when he's desperately worried, he seems only marginally different from when he's ecstatically happy. I would have found it astounding that my brother hadn't known this about our father if I hadn't been so maxed out on astonishment: How could he have not felt the violence in our house? Yet sometimes in adulthood, those memories so far behind me, I've wondered if I had imagined it all. Had it been so bad? Had it even happened at all? The memory of being hurt by someone you love is dangerous to return to, and perhaps just as dangerous to forget, and as I sat there with my brother—the sibling who moved back to Mississippi to run the family business—I wondered if he would have made different choices for himself and his young family if he had known this story.

It would have been around the same time as the lawsuit, my brother said.

What lawsuit?

You didn't know about the lawsuit?

I didn't know about the lawsuit, didn't know that our father had punched one of his employees—in self-defense, he attested—and that when that employee sued, and when it seemed the case would go to trial, our mother was asked to be a character witness, and she told them that if she were a character witness, she would have to tell the truth, so they settled out of court.

The first thing I remember wanting to be, at seven, was far from Mississippi, and though I accomplished this goal early, it would take longer to understand that I would never be very far from this place. My brother's kitchen is in the house where our father grew up, where our grandfather was born and died, where our great-grandfather lived, where even our great-great-grandfather lived before he died and was buried one block away. Only a child would ever have the hope that she could ever entirely get away from such a thing.

My grandfather was never more loving than on his death-bed. He wanted to kiss all his grandchildren. He forgave my mother for having divorced his son. He believed his nurse to be his wife, his lifelong and loyal wife with whom he had shared an intense love all these decades, and he died, quite happily married to Marsha the nurse, just a few yards away from where he'd been born in 1920.

At some point during the spring that I told Peter we needed to get divorced because I was in love with The Reason, he asked me to imagine what I would think about this decision from the vantage point of my deathbed.

Right before he asked this, I could still see the possibility of staying together, of pushing myself to uphold the agreements I'd made with him, and refusing to be in love with The Reason. But then he'd asked me to picture myself on my deathbed, and it was entirely clear—I had to leave. For several months before this breaking point, I'd begun to feel that my hesitance about pregnancy was not just a fear of something I truly wanted but was plainly a sign that childbirth was not and never had been something I could imagine myself doing. Peter and I had been talking this through since Christmas, his confidence unwavering that my fear would pass, that our life together would continue as planned. Once I even asked him if we could agree that if it was clear that I didn't want a baby after I had one that he would take our kid and let me go. He calmly told me this would not happen. *But you can't be sure of that*, I challenged. He assured me that he could be sure, that he was sure.

What will you think about this from your deathbed? My husband's wants had been consistent—to get married, to stay married, to have a child—while mine had become clear the hard way. I had, like so many fools before me, gotten right up to the edge of one life in order to learn I had to run in the opposite direction. If I had been more like him, maybe the deathbed question would have made me stay, but I wasn't, so I left.

A good death, I said to Sara, breaking a morning silence over the kitchen table.

I was just thinking that, she said. *I was just about to say that.*

I'd woken up feeling like we'd even had the same dreams, the shared consciousness of living together blending in the night. Sara's father was dying, and one of her longest running friendships was dying, and neither was experiencing a good death. Daily, we craved good death. Our cravings remained unmet.

That morning I couldn't stop thinking about the winter I'd learned to quilt from CB, the same winter I'd tried to reread the Bible. My patience for the Bible was thin, but I could sit with CB sewing by hand for hours. We didn't have a machine. We could have gotten one, but the point of our quilting wasn't to get it done quickly. The point of the quilting was never quite the quilt.

Around the same time, I had talked about my childhood extremism in a radio interview during lockdowns, and my mother called to gently say that perhaps the way I had read the Bible as a kid had been a bit reductive. I agreed. *Yet it seems to me the book was designed to reduce the reader*, I didn't quite say.

I ultimately failed to reread the Bible, but I did complete a baby blanket that winter—irregular but sincere, fit to be puked upon by the twins my sister-in-law gave birth to in that hopeful first month of 2020. I sent it to them a year later, having still not met them, crying as I watched their first birthday party on a grainy Zoom call.

Before the twins turned two, I quit sewing, leaving the loose beginnings of a full-size quilt behind. Without CB's company, I knew I'd be unable to work on it. The incomplete project was a large swath of beige flannel and muslin connected with a few lumpy, concentric arcs, an intricate trapunto that I'd undertaken knowing I was out of my depth.

I also left the tomato pin cushion and wooden cigar box of needles and thread she'd given me when we began to sew together.

You can finish it if you want, I wrote in my last note to her, *or dismantle it for the fabric.* I wonder what she did with it, but I know she probably just threw it all away, as she would sometimes impulsively trash something that upset her. Often it was a soup she'd made that didn't turn out right. *Ah, fuck,* she'd mutter, then pour the soup directly into our compost in the backyard. It became a running joke in the house—CB and her ill-fated soups—but I was also charmed by her propensity to say to hell with it, to curse the day that butternut squash ever arrived, to go out for a burger, to eat it happily.

I'd based my ambitious quilt off a photograph she'd shown me of a Scottish rendition of that traditional Italian technique, textured with circular ripples of fill, like the texture of a pond after a stone's been dropped in. I knew that my version of it would turn out ghostly and imperfect, like most things I love.

CB's apartment in our house had also been ghostly and imperfect. I wanted to remodel her kitchen and install built-in shelves for all her books. I drew up plans and priced out wood for the latter—floor to ceiling, hidden brackets, painted the same white as the walls. Built-in shelves are the sign of someone who isn't moving anytime soon, I thought. A big reason we'd bought the house was to have her near, to give her a yard, no landlords, a sense of a stable future, privacy without too much solitude. I spent many evenings at her kitchen table up there, drinking wine and talking shit.

Sometimes we conspired about The Reason, trading information we knew the other needed, and often I asked her to tell the story of getting kicked out of a convent, simply too much for the nuns, having to flee in the night. She told me about her life before her husband and first son died as their photographs watched us. I felt I knew them both—Chip and Abram. That I had the same birthday as her first son was a point of pride, as if I were really some mirror child of hers, born elsewhere, finding her now.

After the novelty and the initial dread had worn off living without most of the obligations I'd once had, I woke up on a table in a bright room in a small house atop a steep hill. Michal's home. Michal was there. A gauzy portrait of Jesus looked over us from the corner. A portrait of Lao-tzu hung beside him. I had been crying, it seemed.

The decision to see Michal was impulsive on purpose. If I had considered it for too long, there would have been reasons not to accept the kind of care she offered, but I had made it my task that winter to do anything I had previously believed myself not to be the type of person to do, activities or gestures I would have foreclosed before beginning, or judged without knowing. They were smallish things, mostly: bong hits with Sean, a tie-dye bikini, slipping my phone number to a stranger, calling the energy healer—but there were larger ones, too: asking for help, writing from life, learning a new language, and this—putting myself in the hands of someone like Michal, without cynicism or detachment but out of a curiosity I found almost frightening.

When Michal asked what place spirituality had in my life, I told her I had no idea anymore, though what I might have meant was that I had no vocabulary or framework that felt adequate. There was that deeply religious childhood, then confusion, then a big nothing, and in the last several years I had become even more hardened to anything immaterial. I'd been warned away from everything New Age as a kid—the work of the devil—and I had avoided it as an adult, too, because it seemed just as rife with manipulation and orthodoxy as organized religion.

But I was putting all that hesitance aside. I was entertaining the possibility that I had been wrong about everything because it seemed most likely that I was, indeed, wrong about nearly everything about which I'd once been so sure. Michal, orphaned in Israel and wandering since she was young, had been in Oaxaca for twenty years, living simply, sewing and selling linen clothing, charging modestly for these sessions. There seemed to be little orthodoxy to what she did. She pulled from various traditions, knew no boundaries or borders. She did not insist upon the authority of her work, but rather she had faith in her interest, her patience, her ability to pay close attention.

What happened in the hours I spent in that white room evades my understanding. I cannot explain with any confidence what it was or what she did or what we did. I would lie on her table and we would enter a kind of shared trance—a slow, somatic experience that either stirred or coincided with a sense of narrative and clarity. I could say I felt this way because I wanted to feel this way; I could dismiss those hours by saying my body had created the experience it needed. A somatic theater. That still doesn't explain it.

I spent three hours at a time on that table with my eyes closed while Michal stood over me, sometimes holding my neck or wrist, sometimes hovering her hands over my body as sensations arose and fell—a tightening, a hard flex, a sharp pain. Often my right bicep trembled and fluttered uncontrollably, and one time it lasted so long that my elbow became sore as if I'd spent a whole day sledgehammering stone. Michal put her hands there, and the pain warmed, then cooled, then vanished completely. Most of these sensations came with thoughts, or half thoughts, or images. When she asked me what I was thinking of, I never knew how I was going to reply, yet everything I said felt both surprising and inevitable, like those sudden statements that come after being uncoiled for months or years in a therapist's office.

A year later, when a friend told me about going to somatic therapy, it seemed that this was what Michal was doing on instinct, somehow uncovering information I'd stored in my body as if smoking a rabbit out of her burrow.

I don't know if you're open to seeing things this way, Michal said one morning, *but you're carrying some entities—would you be interested in me removing them?*

Somehow I had not been expecting anything like this, anything so specifically supernatural, but I suppose I also hadn't been expecting anything in particular, which of course makes room for everything. This is the trouble with pushing yourself to go places you wouldn't normally go—even there, all the way out *there*, there is an even deeper out there. Yet I could not deny that this time with Michal already seemed to be helping me, insofar as I could understand it. I had been sleeping. I felt lighter, easier in the unrecognizable shape my life had taken. I was more honest, more patient. I had said things aloud to her that I hadn't been able to say alone or to anyone else.

So—*yes*, I told her, *do what you will to the entities*.

A few days later I lay on my back on the floor of her living room as she drummed, rhythmically and methodically, for more than two hours. At first I felt nothing but foolish, then a little tired, then I started hearing things, then I started feeling my chest caving in, then flexing out, then a tensing and arching in the abdomen, and my neck seemed to have lengthened, and I started to hum involuntarily, and I sensed my face contorting, and toward the end of this process everything was still and soft except my left index finger: it moved wildly, as if tracing a rapid cursive in the air.

How do you feel? she asked, after it was over.

I was absolutely dazed, and later I would wonder if I'd simply been hypnotized by the drumming, if that was all it was. In every study I later read about hypnosis, the scientists agreed it was a real and measurable mental phenomenon, but that it was completely, still, a mystery. The research I found about cognitive trance more than a year later explained a bit more, but mainly raised even more complex questions.

Finally replying to her, I told Michal I felt like I was pregnant, though I'd never been pregnant and did not want to be pregnant. Then she explained, in the most matter-of-fact way, that she and Jesus and Lao-tzu had conducted a spiritual surgery on me. They had cut open my abdomen and removed a diseased, lost soul that had slipped into my body somewhat recently, as I had been all too emotionally vulnerable these past few months. Then, Michal said, she had traveled to the underworld, dug up some dirt, and filled my wound with it. That must be, she said, why I felt pregnant. It was the dirt from the underworld.

I found this summary of the two previous hours absolutely bizarre and so outside my understanding of reality that I had no idea how to reply. Yet it was undeniable that something had happened in my body and to my consciousness that defied almost everything I knew about having a body and a consciousness. After a long silence I admitted, somewhat shyly, that I hadn't realized Jesus was going to be involved.

He is one of my guides, Michal said. She spoke of Jesus as if he were her roommate, her left leg, her middle name, someone she'd been so close to for so long she barely thought of him as the son of God, our Lord and Savior. Or maybe she didn't think of him that way. Maybe she knew Jesus from somewhere else. It was like she'd brought up some long-lost boyfriend of mine and I was wondering if he even remembered me.

When we took the spirit out, it was a very old man wearing red pants, she continued, laughing. *It was really weird.*

But the demon, she explained, *was a common variety.* Black fur. Small. She'd easily taken it out of my right leg. A demon. OK. It was news to me that I had been carrying a demon around.

Yet whatever did or did not happen in that room, I trusted, at least, that Michal believed it, saw it, that this is the world she lives in, the world she sees. I never saw a demon or a diseased soul, but I don't believe it is demeaning to the immediate calm I felt that afternoon to call this all, perhaps, a work of theater or fiction.

Fiction is a record of what has never happened and yet absolutely happened, and those of us who read it regularly have been changed and challenged and broken down a thousand times over by those nothings, changed by people who never existed doing things that no one quite did, changed by characters that don't entirely exist and the feelings and thoughts that never exactly passed through them.

Emotion, too, is invisible, and not reliably measured or quantified, but we are moved by it all the same. Is an emotion any more or less real than that little furry demon? This is an honest question, though I also cannot easily accept the idea of an invisible *demon* having slipped into my body and needing to be removed. What she saw as a demon, maybe I would see as an anger, a resentment, a long-clutched guilt. At most, a religious service might change its attendants, just as art can change its viewers, and perhaps the thing that religion and art share is that mysterious progression: the emotional and visceral process of one idea breaking down to make way for the entrance of another.

Months later in Manhattan I went to see Heather Christian's *Oratorio for Living Things*, an opera, essentially, about being alive. With hardly a division between audience and stage, the choir wandered the room, singing with the athleticism and possession of the spiritually devout. Some of the pieces were in Latin, others were constructed of the testimony of strangers, people who submitted memories to Christian to use as libretto. I hadn't known what to expect when I bought tickets to celebrate Brenda's and my April birthdays, since I knew she was also an ardent fan of Heather Christian. I sat between my friend and a stranger with my mouth hanging open for ninety minutes, trembling, weeping at I don't even know what, and I left the theater both a different person and the same person, or rather I left feeling more myself than I had when I had entered.

Every Good Friday as a child, I cried when the church went dark, and I was sure my grief was an outgrowth of my faith. Or you could say it was the hypnosis of poetry, or an experience of fiction in its purest form. On Good Friday we left the church in darkness, and we had to live the rest of that day and the next in that symbolic darkness. On Easter Sunday we could come back and retrieve the light that had been purposefully hidden from us. Denied, then indulged— I left the sanctuary on Easters feeling more regenerated than ever, from the soles of my feet to my eyelids.

In California in the middle of the night I told D about the demon, the man in the red pants, and all the embarrassing, strange things that happened with Michal. We've been close friends for many years, and I wasn't afraid he'd think of me as crazy or foolish, but I expected, at least, that he'd be surprised. He was not.

Oh, you had an exorcism, he said.

I hadn't been using that word for it, but yes, I admitted, it seems that I did, that I had, that I'd been exorcised.

It turns out that D, quite by accident, had experienced something similar some years back, but he hadn't told almost anyone about his experience since he, like I, still slightly disbelieved it. He hadn't previously thought of himself as someone interested in such things, but after trying what felt like everything else to treat his anxiety around public speaking, D ended up seeing a hypnotherapist who, at the start of their first meeting, listed out the possible roots of anxiety—*It might be trauma you haven't dealt with, or it might be a matter of self-esteem, or issues with your parents, or in very rare cases there's a ghost living in your body*—and at this moment he surprised himself when he began to cry, a crying that came from some deep and mysterious shame, and the hypnotherapist looked up from her papers—*Why are you crying? Can you tell me why?* An hour later the hypnotherapist had removed a ghost from his body (an older, female ghost who was apparently quite angry) in a process that D called an exorcism, and with the ghost his anxiety, too, had gone away.

And there we were, two grown-ups prone to cynicism, two stubborn writers who've long tended toward doing everything alone; there we were holding each other in a dim apartment, admitting we really had no idea what the body is, what death is, what emotions are, how anything really works at all. I had to laugh, and he had to laugh, then we both had to stop laughing.

I spent the last decade using fiction as the treatment for anything that ailed me, but for months after leaving Chicago I had no use for it—not as a reader and not as a writer—and though I eased back into reading it again, writing it had remained beside the point. While having dinner with Sara I wondered if I stopped writing stories because living felt so fictional that writing fiction had become unnecessary—keeping track of a day was enough.

Later that night Sara told me something her father had told her about his time in Vietnam. He'd been taken as a prisoner of war and kept in a cage half-submerged in a river. He'd been forced by his captors to play Russian roulette with a loaded gun and survived only because the base was air raided by the Americans; in the melee, he'd escaped.

I scoffed. I'd seen that film before.

So you knew it was a lie?

Of course not, Sara said. She believed it quite naturally: *He was my father. I was a child.* Her father had always been recalcitrant and inconsistent, and this war story had a way of explaining or excusing his impenetrability as a parent.

It was years later when Sara watched the film *The Deer Hunter* on an airplane, on a lark, that she recognized her father's story as nearly identical—the cage, the roulette, the unlikely escape.

And then *you knew it was a lie?*

Again she told me she had not. It's natural for a child to want to trust their parents, though it was eerie to see it like that, this story he had told her for so long now dramatized by actors, but the idea that her father might have passed this narrative off as his own, that he might have lied to her so directly—it was not a notion she was willing to accept.

Several more years passed before her PhD in psychology took Sara to a veteran's hospital where another therapist mentioned that the military kept records of who had been imprisoned in Vietnam, data that was available to the public now. She looked up her father's name. It wasn't there.

Five minutes before she told me all this, Sara and I were both flirting with the waiter, ordering girly cocktails, but when he came by again I stared at a wall and Sara was the one to smile and say, *We're fine.*

I never met Sara's father but I already knew he had failed my friend in significant enough ways that I long ago wrote him off as a villain. But he was also *her* villain, the villain she did not choose, the angry man in her house who she would necessarily have to account for, somehow, some way.

All my friends had been angry when I told them about the email The Reason had sent from the other room, but no one had been shocked, as this seemed consistent with the impenetrable and self-contained person they knew him to be. I had been shocked because I knew a different person, just as Sara knew a different father, as there is really no other way to live in a house with such a man, as life cannot work without love and love cannot work without trust, or belief, no matter how unearned it may be.

Still—a trust betrayed is always a shock. That is the hazard of trust.

A stray kitten arrived one night at my cabin in a grubby beach town and adopted me as her mistress. I named her Banana Bread.

It was the first time I had a relationship with an animal on my own. She wasn't a family pet or a partner's pet. Banana Bread and I had no context for one another, no additional relationships to reflect or complicate ours. She had come to my yard by her own random will and stayed because I paid attention to her and fed her—first a crumbled piece of banana bread, and later the cat food I bought for her at the bodega.

At first she was a spectacle in my otherwise quiet life, but after I spent a few mornings with her sleeping against my legs as I worked, and after I used a broom to chase away some loose dogs who had crawled under our fence and scared her, and after I realized that my first thought every morning was of Banana Bread and how immediately I would go onto the porch to whisper her name and how pleased I was when she appeared, I understood my relationship with her had ceased to be purely circumstantial.

One night Banana Bread climbed through a hole in the fence as I was coming home late, mewing—tender and pleading. It was the first time since she arrived that I'd been out late, and I assumed she was hungry, but there was food and water in her bowls on the porch, and that night she sat purring in my lap; it was beginning to seem that she really did prefer my company to its absence, though I also suspected this was a gross anthropomorphism.

I began to look up vets in the area, and asked my local friends if they'd take her in when I left town, saying I'd come back for her once I had a plan of where to live, what to do, and it was then that Banana Bread, seeming to sense my attempts at possession, vanished.

Don't panic, I thought, *don't worry. She is a cat and I am a person who feeds her. She'll come back.* I kept putting out the kibble, but it stayed there all day. I kept calling her name every dim morning, but she never appeared.

A February in New Orleans many years ago, Sara and I found a peacock, loose, standing on someone's front yard. We stared at his fanned feathers in awe until he suddenly folded himself away and scurried behind a house just as a woman came out onto her front porch. Timidly, we asked, *Was that your peacock?* She seemed to consider the question quite seriously. *Who? Big Bird? No, he's his own person.* She told us he'd just arrived one day, that he wasn't anyone's, and I tried to remember this woman, how she kept a reasonable distance from that animal, even if she had named him.

Eventually some of my neighbor's free-ranging chickens found the kibble. Then the dogs came. Then I stopped putting it out except overnight, but every morning it was the same—untouched food, maybe a fly dead in the water.

I gave up, or at least I told myself I'd given up; in fact, I did not stop looking for the cat around town and calling her name in the mornings and squinting every time I saw another stray in the distance. This was, I believed, just a matter of curiosity and not a habit of misplaced attachment. Banana Bread had not been my pet. We barely knew each other. She had always just been passing through. Be reasonable.

And anyway I was in town only for another three weeks, and I had no monopoly on cat food, and Banana Bread—charming and social—she likely knew plenty of homes where other people were happy to feed her. In fact, perhaps my cabin was just a vacation from some other, better, stable home. A local. The real thing.

What would Seneca say? *The best compromise between love and good sense is both to feel longing and to conquer it.* Yet it is irritating to see love framed in opposition to good sense.

Some weeks later over dinner with Sara in a restaurant with a sand floor, I suddenly thought of the cat and how I wished Sara had met her. We'd been in a particularly good mood—holding hands and laughing and winking at people we didn't know—but the mention of Banana Bread bent me over with tears.

Oh, but hadn't I been feeling so great lately? I'd been having such a good time. And what about all the sex I'd been having and the fifteen new versions of an orgasm I'd found with that kind of annoying person who'd just done the tantra workshop? Didn't that count for anything? So what if I had been demolished? So what if I had no particular home at the moment? There were good ways to be demolished, good ways to be untethered, and now I am the only one who tells me what to do. A demon and a diseased soul were taken out of my body. There are no walls in my life. Oh look at all these extreme feats of freedom. Do you remember that peacock we saw in that yard in New Orleans, Sara? Where do you think he is now? I am my own person, too. I am crying at a communal table in a Thai restaurant by the ocean. I am enjoying everything. Nothing's hidden anymore. I don't mind telling anyone anything. Is everyone's trouble quite the same? Isn't this the way? Isn't it all so easy now?

In my mid-twenties I kept a secret list of everything a strange man ate or drank during our nights and mornings together. *Sancerre, sushi, coffee, granola.* I must have thought keeping track of this might help me understand who he was and what he wanted, subjects that always eluded me.

Some lines from William Gass's *On Being Blue* later explained to me the impulse beneath that weird inventory: *Love is a nervous habit. Haven't many said so? Snacking. Smoking. Talking. Joking. Alike as light bulbs. Drinking. Drugging. Frigging. Fucking. Writing. Forgetting. Nerves. Nerves, nerves, nerves.*

Now I know he was just a person looking for something and never finding it. It wasn't me; it wasn't anyone. The last thing I ever saw him eat, he later told me, he threw up.

In the winter I read the most wintery line by Sarah Manguso: *Elegies are the best love stories because they're the whole story.* Which is to say that the moment you really learn who you married is when you divorce them or that the last real test of parenthood is becoming your child's child.

I took a photograph of The Reason every time I saw him on an escalator—in airports, public transit, the grocery store, a mall, one pharmacy, and elsewhere, all over the world. I've since deleted this collection.

Weil, of course, offers no consolation:

Love is a sign of our wretchedness . . . It is God who in love withdraws from us so that we can love him.

But I cannot bend entirely to her vision of God, nor of love. She had these terrible headaches all her life, Simone Weil did, and sometimes it seems she thought the headaches were the very presence of God. She lived only one life. So do we all. But if she'd had lived past her thirties, how many of her ideas could have gained layers?

Then, on a grim spring day, I came across a passage by Thomas Merton:

Life curves upward to a peak of intensity, a high point of value and meaning, at which all its latent creative possibilities go into action and the person transcends himself or herself in encounter, response and communion with another. It is for this that we came into the world—this communion and self-transcendence. We do not become fully human until we give ourselves to each other in love.

And I wondered if I had ever lived up to this idea, and I wondered, if not, if I'd live long enough to find a way to live up to it.

For a while all my conversations seem to keep returning to the word "spiritual."

How strange it feels to need that word now after rolling my eyes at it for so long. Sean comes over to Sara's with coffee one morning, and we all talk about meditation and ecstatic states and a particular kind of quiet we've both felt that resists description. It's a puzzle we can't solve, a new verse in the conversation we've been having for twenty years.

In the spring around a long table with writers from all over the world, we passed around the question of how religion or its absence affects or disaffects the spiritual state of being a child.

Childhood is inherently mystical—we all agreed on this—a natural awe that comes with having more questions than answers, but that innocence is so easily flattened by the rigidity of religion. Most of us grew up going to a church or cathedral with varying degrees of intensity. Some of us still held a loose grip on Christianity, but most of us had defected entirely, leaving families to their orthodoxy. One of us—Susana, the most unusual—spent her childhood among Portuguese anarchists who derided organized religion, despised marriage, saw it all as a trap and a lie. The most rebellious thing she could have done was to get married or find God, which she never did.

I felt intensely jealous of Susana's intellectual and political education as opposed to all the time I spent focused on the ancient morality and monomyth of the Bible.

A friend once told me he felt we could talk for hours

and there would always be something he didn't understand about me.

It must be my Christian soul, I said without hesitation, surprising myself.

To hell with it, I say some days, and *Oh let me keep it*, I say on others.

The word "spiritual" is an irritant in all this, not quite the right word but not quite the wrong one. We all suspect we need it anyway, though we don't really like the word anymore, if we ever did, and we can't say much more for its derivations—*"spirituality," "spirit"*—as it seems they've all gone brittle from overuse or misuse around us. Can we get this word back from the churches we no longer belong to? Can we get it back from the Yoga Industrial Complex, and from the gurus, and the marketing departments, and our Catholic educations, and those people who so loudly profess detachment from things to which they are quite clearly attached? We want to speak of gnosis and mysticism without our phones listening to us and populating browser ad space with advertisements for Goddess Retreats and bogus supplements and acupuncture mats.

We want to talk about something—something just beyond the material, something about love and trust, something about something we don't have words for. We try to keep trying. We try not to laugh at ourselves. We are trying to find a way to meet each other somewhere outside of what we can see.

———

It seemed to Zac that many of his otherwise rationally minded friends—*scientists, even literal scientists*—had started putting their trust in superstitious abstractions. A Sagittarius moon, the Devil card, or the color of their sacral chakras—any of these things could affect their behavior, sometimes radically changing the trajectory of their families, relationships, or careers.

How could a rational person really do this? Zac asked me and Haroula and Oliver as we watched a spring afternoon drain away on the deck. *How could anyone put so much trust in mutable symbols and images? And wasn't it exactly this—huge portions of the country putting their faith in outright lies—that had just caused and continued to cause us so much damage, so much strife, so much death?*

When we tried to answer his questions, we found ourselves outmatched by even larger questions. Haroula and Oliver had just gotten engaged, a gesture also suffused with symbolism and faith. When I had gotten engaged a decade prior, my friend Filip had called it, memorably, "*going public with risk.*" Many years later, as Filip came down from Milwaukee to drive the U-Haul I was too afraid to drive in Chicago, I knew I would forever remember the sight of crumbling row houses we drove past as he said everyone lived their lives first and wrote the narratives for them afterward, an idea that reminded me of the night in Roma Sur that Amado had defined humans, offhand, as *metaphoric animals*. Symbolism is both hollow and solid, a crutch, yes, but what's so wrong with needing help to get around?

As a girl in a church pew, nothing was more beautiful and more affecting to me than watching a baptism. Often the babies cried or looked terrified as they were carried up to the altar, and I always hoped that once the water was poured over their bald heads that they'd become placid, and when they did, I thought, *That's God doing that,* and when they didn't, I thought, *That's just babies doing what they do.*

I loved getting swept up in the story, the hope, the physical feeling of God's regeneration happening live and in person, in sermons and baptisms and hymns and church. I loved it just as much as I loved theater and reading. I loved it from what seems, now, to be the exact same place in my body.

There on the deck, however, Zac still looked quite serious. Zac grew up in what he called a *tepid Judaism.* He plays piano for a living, the only job he's ever had, as being a pianist was what he wanted from a young age, a desire and ambition he never questioned. Having a directionality that intense, to me, is as difficult to imagine as my childhood faith must be to him.

As we talked it seemed, again, that orthodoxy was the only real thing to be feared in any of this, and maybe it was the infinite mutability and the flexibility of interpretation that made things like astrology and tarot (but also art and literature and psychology) so appealing.

One definition of orthodoxy: a tightly held belief that a certain story cannot change or should not change or simply will not change. Another definition: the angry man in your house.

And yet, I wondered aloud to Zac and our friends, *placing one's trust only in what can be totally proven is just another kind of orthodoxy.*

Still—we didn't like where this left us. To the extent that I found utility in my experiences with Michal, I had to accept their inherent nebulousness. I had to accept, even, that she or I or both of us might be totally deluded, that I may still be that girl looking glassy-eyed at the just-baptized baby.

Our last autumn together The Reason and I were walking in Chicago when an odd silence settled between us. I asked him what he was thinking; he said he was having a conversation with me. *About what*, I wanted to know, but he didn't say; he already knew my thoughts on the matter, he said.

During my nightly prayers as a child I sometimes ran out of things to pray, and I felt so sure that He knew what I would have told Him if I could have conjured it. By lying there in His gaze, my devotion became clear and perfect; I was not just a tired child, lacking anything to pray about, but an immaculate being, so full of faith there wasn't room for anything else.

In errata, Keats noted that *one of the most mysterious of semi-speculations is, one would suppose, that of one Mind's imagining into another.* (*One would suppose*, he wrote, as if Keats was hesitating to be sure what Keats was truly thinking.)

But it must have been pleasurably familiar to have my unspoken thoughts intuited then privately extruded through the many reasons of The Reason. It must have reminded me of God.

However satisfying writing is—that mix of discipline and miracle, which leaves you in control, even when what appears on the page has emerged from regions beyond your control—it is a very poor substitute indeed for the joy and agony of loving.

The philosopher Gillian Rose wrote this in her last complete book before she died of ovarian cancer, but I didn't know anything about Rose when I picked up the copy of *Love's Work* that Sara had left in the living room. I was awake early that day, glad to be alone but also wondering how long I was going to be this glad to be alone. As if it was urgent business I needed to take care of, I surrendered most of the day to this short, circuitous mediation on love and death and sex and longing.

There is no democracy in any love relation: only mercy. To be at someone's mercy is dialectical damage . . . You may be less powerful than the whole world, but you are always more powerful than yourself.

Several times I had to put the book down and lie on the floor. Blaming the late June heat and the questions Rose was raising, I was unable to get dressed until well past noon. It was the first summer I'd been single in a decade, and though the sex I'd been having was easily the best I'd ever had, I felt emotionally shrink-wrapped, always prepared to expect less than nothing from the people I'd been spending time with.

This, too, was *a very poor substitute for the joy and agony of loving.*

Part of what terrified me about the idea of loving another person again was how easy it has been for me to misdiagnose abject mistreatment as simply misexpressed love. I had loved The Reason with a faith I knew to be profound, and now I knew the *dialectical damage* this had cost me. His sudden, casual suggestion that I didn't love him at all had forbid me from doing so; I feared it had also damaged my capacity to ever experience such a faith again. This left me with an intimate life that felt divided: the safety of platonic love, and the false intimacy of sex with people I barely knew. I wasn't sure if I agreed with this version of my life, but it had begun to seem to be the only option.

A fear of misunderstanding is also what's led me to cut nearly every sex scene I've ever written from the final text of a novel or story. A reader couldn't be blamed for assuming that the person who wrote my novels had no sexual life at all, or at least no opinion on the existence of sex, that she may have taken all acts of intercourse silently, motionless, that she had simply watched them happening to her with a series of rote and remote glances.

I've felt a pressure not to depict sex in my fiction, not to get too specific—doing otherwise, it's implied, will broadcast a certain image or run the risk of subsuming the rest of the narrative. But it is possible to be particular about sex without being graphic or betraying anyone's privacy, and given the way that our sexual lives can end up having such an effect on the direction of the rest of our lives, why would any writer avoid it? I've never entirely trusted the notion that sex scenes are often poorly written; it seems the lens has been clouded with our anxieties, prejudices, and latent squeamishness about those private narratives being made public.

William Gass wrote about this dilemma in *On Being Blue*, but if he was suggesting any specific criteria a writer might apply to a story's more carnal moments, I could never discern his advice.

> *An author is responsible for everything that appears in his books. If he claims that reality requires his depiction of the sexual, in addition to having a misguided aesthetic, he is a liar, since we shall surely see how few of his precious pages are devoted to chewing cabbage, hand-washing, sitting on the stool, or, if you prefer, filling out forms, washing floors, cheering teams . . . The sexual, in most works, disrupts the form.*

But is it the *sexual* that disrupts the form, or is it our nervy perception of the sexual that disrupts form? Reality at large has never been my subject, but interiority always has been. The interiority of a person filling out forms or sitting on the stool or chewing cabbage or fucking may or may not illuminate something of value of that character; the answer comes only in context. A description of a sexual act need not be an attempt at realist totality, but rather an opportunity to explore the variation of consciousness that happens in intimacy, a profound interruption of our default state of being corporeally isolated.

Love-making is never simply pleasure, Gillian Rose wrote. *The sexual exchange will be as complicated as the relationship in general—even more so. Kiss, caress and penetration are the relation of the relation . . . The three I harbor—body, soul, and Paraclete—press against the same triplicity in you.*

And it seems not to be coincidental that I've had trouble writing (and therefore trouble thinking) about spirituality concurrent to the years I've flatly avoided writing anything about sex.

When writing moves on its own authority, it has the same inevitability of good sex. Not much thought is given to what sentence comes next, to where to put this or that hand, to what to do with your mouth. My hands, when the writing is going well, seem to be animated by my subconscious, just as they do when the fucking is going well. One subconscious touching another subconscious—perhaps it's never more than that.

On impulse one night with trusted friends who knew how, I got tied up and whipped for no reason other than I'd never done such a thing, and if your sweet friends can't beat you with kitchen implements, who will? Who will kiss you, who will push aside your shirt and suck the flesh above your heart, who will ask for more rope, who will show you how to transform love into force back into love, who will tighten the knots into an ecstatic sense of knowing you're in the right place, of being exactly, precisely, entirely within your limited body?

For months I'd been juggling these conflicting appetites:

the desire to be unequivocally free and the desire for some kind of boundary, some kind of limitation to constrain my life. I want to be both protected from and given totally to the anything and everything I was now allowed. I wanted to be in love with one person, to feel that kind of faith again, but it was never the right time, never the right person. Somehow being tied up for an hour had been a rite in all this, the chaos of having more freedom than I knew what to do with.

When I texted Avery about it the next morning, and she wrote back: *Doesn't it feel like being held?*

Gass said it best: *Nowhere do we need order more than at any orgy.*

Would it feel like this if our native languages were the same? Daniel asked in the first days we were falling in love, and later I wondered if the very concept of a native language was a ruse, given how many things a person can feel that never make the leap into words, thought-ghosts floating beneath everything we try to say to one another. What good had lingual fluency ever done for me when it came to love? *I feel like I'm getting away with something,* I had told him, though what I meant was I felt something for which I had no words. *What is this?* he asked me all afternoon, all evening, that night, and the next morning, though I think he meant he knew exactly what this was.

I kept thinking of a phrase I didn't really understand—

Feeling speaks only to feeling. This idea (a command, almost) had been trailing me since I first read it in Ludwig Feuerbach's *The Essence of Christianity* in the guest bedroom at my mother's house in late spring. I didn't know why I was reading that book; maybe I was just looking for something to be angry about, craving the way anger turns the contrast up on a day. Logical arguments in favor of faith used to reliably make me angry, but it didn't seem to work anymore. *Feeling speaks only to feeling.* I felt I'd rescued this sentence from Feuerbach, kidnapped it into a new use.

Language is always a translation of emotion; it's possible for physical intimacy to be a push backward, a re-arrival to the pure meaning of love without its translation into words. The simplicity of kissing—something that does nothing, accomplishes nothing—estranges us from a need for language, and when such desire is commonly held, it's commonly felt: feeling speaking to feeling. Anything outside that communion falls away.

One subconscious touching another subconscious, I had tried to say, but it came out unsteadily: *Our subconscious-ness-es?* The plural wouldn't cooperate with my tongue. *Could you say, subconsci?* We laughed. It was just language, which meant it was never enough, like all addictions.

Later, taking a break from the common ground of English, I spoke my brittle Spanish like a confused, shy child, humbled to be so lost in words, the one tool I'd always used to help me find my way.

On a cool white floor on that hot day, Daniel's hands on

my back, I said to him, *I can't find a way to comprehend how to explain how good that feels*, and he said, *Don't*.

Before our house was publicly listed, an offer came in through the real estate agent from a developer who wanted to knock it down. A 134-year-old home with strange storefront windows and no serious problems—landmarked and beautiful and loved—one of the last unusual structures for blocks in every direction. A total demolition would obviously be bad for the neighborhood, the environment, for beauty itself, for the city, and even though the idea of that home had already been destroyed for me, and even though I knew I would never see it again, the idea of it being literally demolished was unsettling.

On our many walks in Chicago The Reason often pointed to new construction and recounted, in mourning, of what had been there before—something decrepit but beautiful, a strange building, an old tree, a derelict field. We were, I felt, united against the act of razing the unusual to make room for the standard. What could be more hideously capitalistic than that? What could be more opposed to what we found meaningful in the world?

I told the real estate agent I had no price for this, that I would not consent to sell the house to anyone who wanted only the lot; the agent told me he understood, that he could imagine the house still had emotional value to me, and the matter of selling a house is always quite complicated, but he had to mention, at least, that The Reason was entertaining the offer—he needed them only to increase the price.

I had painted the walls in the kitchen, the living room, the library, including the interiors of each of the built-in shelves, both offices, three bathrooms, two floors—a process of coating, sanding, re-coating, re-sanding, and sealing them over many days—and I had painted our bedroom a calm gray, painted the insides of two closets and the fronts of a dozen cabinets, and I had built several shelves and structures, hung drywall, hung art, made art, painted a precise white rectangle for film projections, refinished hideous tiles, organized and reorganized closets and tool sheds, deep cleaned the garage, learned basic electrical work to hang three pendant lights, planted an herb garden, harvested garlic, battled with bean vines, and all the while The Reason had watched, approvingly, nodding, and for a certain price he would have seen it all come down under a wrecking ball. That, at least, would have been an ending.

Many years ago I watched a documentary by Michael Kimball and Luca Dipierro called *I Will Smash You*. Kimball had invited strangers off the internet to his home in Baltimore where he showed them to the backyard. There, a table bore several implements of destruction—hammers and garden tools and scissors and the like. Each stranger had brought an object they wanted to destroy with the understanding that they would explain why they wanted to destroy it, then do so, all on camera. The stories were mostly simple, often about heartbreak or bad jobs; more than an object, they'd come to destroy a memory or a failure or a longing. Small electronics and keepsakes and at least one chintzy figurine were destroyed, and at the end a woman in a velvet dress took a crowbar to a car, and all of them had a way of smiling when it was over. *What a relief.*

Adam Robinson, a poet, came to destroy the Protestant hymn *It Is Well with My Soul.* He sang it into the air around him, calmly lifted a baseball bat, and swung it in every direction, not resting until the song had truly been destroyed. It was an ideal poem, I thought, a perfect act of making nothing happen.

One of the last nights I was in the guest room I thought I heard The Reason outside the shut door, calling out my name, my full name, calling it out like a question, but I was in bed and had the covers up to my neck, and I felt sure I was hearing things; then there was a little knock on the door, and I heard his voice still asking for me, so I spoke back.

The Reason?

And there was silence.

The Reason?

And a longer silence this time, a slower one, then nothing, then even less than nothing, then sleep.

Later he told me he had indeed been outside my door, knocking, saying my name. He said he had the sense I wanted to talk to him, so he was coming up to offer what he believed I wanted, but I had nothing else to say to him and did not want to hear from him anymore, perhaps ever again.

Will there be no end to your assumptions about what I want?

I asked him, then I answered my own question: *There will be no end to your assumptions about what I want.*

We, both of us, we had hallucinated the other.

I met Avery at MoMA to see a Matisse exhibit, and she asked me how writing was going, and I asked her how writing was going, and we both admitted it wasn't really going so well lately. Our trouble was a shared one: we were looking for endings, but all we could find was more middle. It was hard, we agreed, to find satisfying conclusions to stories that weren't exactly stories but rather a set of prompts that resisted completion, a Möbius strip of narrative.

I reasoned that our difficulty with endings must have come from the same place—that she and I both tended to work with bottomless questions because we didn't actually want to reach the end of our questioning. We liked our work and felt glad to do it, and maybe we even hid within it, at times, and maybe we enjoyed that hiding, hiding so that we may be found.

Yet books were finite, podcasts were finite, films had last frames, everything has an end or if not an end then at least—sure, OK, fine—a deadline. Couldn't we at least find an adequate phrase or image that didn't feel like a cop-out, a feint, or a compromise? Couldn't we reach an ending that didn't lie about the end?

Was Matisse the original influencer? Avery wryly asked no one in particular while looking at *The Red Studio*. She was asking this because we found ourselves wanting everything he'd depicted. That color, that feeling, that arrangement. There was something about the way he'd framed the space that had compelled or described our desire for it. We wanted the paintings, the sculptures, the whole red room itself.

It just happened that the Venetian red that dominates that famous painting is the red of my dreams, the red I imagine on a floor of an otherwise white room, a room I want to believe I am moving toward though it could be years and years away, a room that either already exists in the world or one I'll have to make. I want to work in that room, I think in my dreams, yes, I want a red studio—or a red-floored studio—or maybe I am just under Matisse's spell, this feeling that I should seek what he sought, the same way a good painting convinces the viewer of the validity of its beauty.

I'd been writing wherever I could for a year by then—in borrowed rooms and atop café tables—and though this was the way I worked all through my twenties, transient, always carrying my desk on my back, I'd become accustomed to being still. My office in Chicago had white walls, white tables, sky-lights, and the peacock-blue floor I spent two weeks refinishing into an oceanic sheen. But that room was over.

The Red Studio was an idealized place for Matisse—a room displaying years of work, an arc of one man's visual language. *I love paintings of paintings*, Avery said, and the moment she named this category, I loved it, too. Books about books. Films about films. Often I find myself writing about an apparent subject that is concealing an almost opposite object. To write about hatred is to see love, vividly. Violence, intimacy. Divinity, humanity. A film about other films will likely end up being a film about life without any cinema at all.

Avery and I looked at one last painting in the exhibit before rushing out at closing time—*Studio under the Eaves*—a depiction of a somber attic where Matisse worked during a period of *"personal and financial troubles,"* as the placard had described it. He couldn't have known that in a few years he would be in his red studio, and he couldn't have known when he painted *The Red Studio*, and no one wanted it and it vanished into obscurity for a time, that years would pass and the canvas would change its meaning.

Ever since I'd left behind my office with the blue floor, I'd been helplessly trying to picture a place for another studio, and yet every temporary space I've used—friend's guest room, hotel bed in Manhattan, K-town sublet, Oaxacan beach, modernist cabin in Switzerland—has had a feeling of permanence while I was there, and in all those places if I was asked where I lived I would say, *Here.*

So it was just the right exhibit to see at just the right time, though Avery had chosen it impulsively, just a reason to wander a vast, air-conditioned space. It had been one of those rare days I'd spent far from my room in Sara's apartment in Brooklyn in exchange for a gridded day in Manhattan—lunch with an editor, picking up the credit card I'd mistakenly left at the Jane, stopping by Brenda's on East Eleventh, then up to the museum. Three subway trips, two long walks, one lunch, one coffee, two glasses of wine. It was the kind of day that, as Avery put it, has a way of drawing a frame around itself. I had moved through so many rooms, so many doors in a single day, and none of them had been mine.

Over wine we talked about self-presentation and self-costume and belonging to a group and the way that New York makes you look at yourself, how it forces you to witness the power of a crowd.

I think you're helping me find my ending, Avery said, so I took a picture of her to put a frame around it, a woman approaching an ending, a woman smiling. Just before we left this Midtown hotel bar, she noticed the framed paintings that had been affixed on the ceiling, looking directly down on us all evening.

When we'd arrived at MoMA and passed through that largest gallery on the second floor, we looked briefly at the Barbara Kruger retrospective, floor to ceiling Kruger-isms. *She's nothing if not consistent,* Avery said, a single sentence that invisibly destroyed every vinyl sticker on every wall, but every time I passed through this particular space I always thought of Marina Abramović sitting there to look at people in 2010, and every time I thought of Abramović, I thought of her artistic breakup with Ulay and their willingness to get completely ceremonial about themselves—the sheer drama of their performance of walking from opposite ends of the Great Wall of China only to meet in the middle to say good-bye forever—and that breakup artwork recalls the dialogue between the writer Carla Lonzi and the sculptor Pietro Consagra, a conversation that the couple had and Lonzi recorded and transcribed and published as a book, *Vai Pure,* titled for the last thing she ever said to him when they broke up and he slipped out the door and left: *Adesso vai pure*, so now you can go.

I had read only a few translated portions of that conversation that had appeared in an essay about Lonzi's work at large. I wanted to read *Vai Pure* in full, but there was no English translation of it, so I asked my friend and Italian translator Teresa if she would read it and tell me anything about it, or maybe consider translating it one day herself. She did me the favor of reading it, but when we met to talk about it, she had to admit, a bit disappointed, that it hadn't really made any sense.

Despite the creep of rain clouds, I hiked out to Punta Cometa to watch the sunset with a stranger named Evy. I'd just met her the night before at the only bar I liked in town; she walked up and asked if this was a good place to make friends. I admired how self-completing this question was. The moment you heard it, the answer was yes.

By the time we reached the beach, dark clouds were approaching, and there was no one on the cliff where a crowd usually gathered each dusk. But Evy was determined, stoic. It was her last night in town, and she'd watched the sunset every night; there was no chance she would miss it. She asked me to take a photograph of her, smiling in her swimsuit in the fine mist of rain, then insisted on taking a few of me as we talked about travel and betrayal and the useful risk of love, and as I look at those pictures now what's most obvious is how a lens has a way of turning a troubled sky beautiful.

Then four naked travelers arrived, singing while they galloped across the sand, undeterred as they ran toward the heavy waves, the howling sea. The sky still threatened a storm, but they didn't seem to mind as they waded into the water. A nearby sign warned, in Spanish and in English, of a dangerous undertow.

The nudists screamed and thrashed, heedless with their bodies as if they were too young to know a broken bone or a medical bill. They let the currents—too strong, it seemed to me—push and pull them, drag them across the sand, suck them outward and spit them back, and eventually the clouds did break, and the sun set in a fury, and those four strangers, drenched and delirious, they deserved that perfect sunset just as they deserved every scrape and bruise that came to them.

Lozano studied the pantry of our absent friend and wondered what she might feed us, Daniel and me, as we came down from the tab of acid we'd split as a first date, hungry and helpless, her children for the evening.

Do you think I can use this? she asked me, holding a jar of artichokes.

Anything removed can be replaced, I said. I meant the jar of artichokes. I meant everything.

Earlier that day I'd learned of more bad news—Michal's home was demolished in a hurricane. Cancers returned and cancers began, and endings again seemed imminent, and plans kept changing. Another friend's marriage fell into divorce, then another, and I kept wondering if it was really true that loss is something quite common in disguise as something unforeseen. But in that calm kitchen, still feeling the urgency of the acid, holding Daniel's hand, I began losing a context that once had felt permanent.

Over dinner, Lozano and Daniel sometimes slipped into Spanish, though I was only beginning to understand it and didn't yet have faith I'd ever speak it with any ease, but I also didn't know that after the summer ended, and after the fall and winter and spring and after another summer came and ended, too, that I would know so many more words than I could have ever imagined needing, and through the convex mirror of another language I would find new capacities to feel faith in another person, fallible as we are, and I didn't know as I ate pizza with my dear friend and this man I barely knew that there was a room in a library thirty blocks north of that apartment where I would ask Daniel a question in Spanish about the future, about how much he was willing to put his faith in something we could not prove, and outside that room in the library there might forever be a cluster of tourists taking pictures of each other with the out-of-commission pay phones, holding the receiver to their faces, smiling as they pretend at the old ways we used to have to reach each other.

ACKNOWLEDGMENTS

Thank you Daniel Saldaña París, Sara Rich, Brenda Cullerton, Brenda Lozano, Sean Brennan, Callie Freeman, Kendra Malone, Maryse Meijer, Wilhelmina Peragine, Filip Tejchman, Jenny Polus, Sarah Manguso, John Vanderslice, Maria Brand, Sammy Loren, Dr. Lozano, Casa Lozano, La Casa Azul, Haroula Rose, Oliver Hill, Christian Stavros, fireplaces, firepits, a certain hammer, John Wray, Sasha Frere-Jones, Isaac Fitzgerald, Kelly Farber, Zac Rae, Amanda Yates Garcia, Kathleen Mackay, Patrick Cottrell, Geoff Dyer, Martin Pousson, Khash Khabushani, Kyp Malone, Francis Farewell Starlite, Patrick deWitt, Tron Miller, Jonathan Lethem, Sarah Ruhl, Paul Holdengräber, Karen Russell, Max Porter, Jim McManus, Emma Lirette, Linda Lirette, Deenah Vollmer, Georgia Bean, my mother, my fathers, my siblings, Chelsea Hodson, Seneca, Tabor Allen, Camila Ibarra, Persephone, Evy, nudity, La Bodega, Augustín, Brian Holder-Chow Lin On, Águila Blanca, Casa Chepil, the pigs, the goats, San Augustinillo, Playa Mermejita, the free-roaming chickens in Mazunte, Banana Bread the cat, Kit Schluter, Golden Teacher, Minhal Baig, Maria Villarreal, Aden Hakimi, U-Haul, Bad Bunny drag night at C'mon Everybody, Greene Avenue, Omi, DW Gibson, Rebecca Novack, Peter Musante, San Cristóbal, poisonous walks under Los Angeles freeways, Cuidad de México, Cuernavaca, La Pitaya, the Jan Michalski Foundation, those dozen hawks who flew outside my window one day, Jason Arthur, Eric Chinski, Jackson Howard, Jin Auh.

WORKS CONSULTED

Alien Tapes, Geo Wyeth; *All About Love*, bell hooks; *Big Time*, Angel Olsen; *The Beauty of the Husband*, Anne Carson; *Bluets*, Maggie Nelson; *Cain Named the Animal*, Shane McCrae; *The Cedars*, John Vanderslice; *Death Jokes*, Amen Dunes; *The Details*, Ia Genberg (translated by Kira Josefsson); *Directions to Myself*, Heidi Julavits; *Easy Beauty*, Chloé Cooper Jones; *Forbidden Notebook*, Alba de Céspedes (translated by Ann Goldstein); *The Freezer Door*, Matilda Bernstein Sycamore; *Gravity & Grace*, Simone Weil (translated by Emma Crawford and Mario von der Ruhr); *In Memory of Memory*, Maria Stepanova (translated by Sasha Dugdale); "In the Desert," Stephen Crane; "It's All Coming Back to Me Now," Céline Dion; *Liars*, Sarah Manguso; *Like a Sky Inside*, Jakuta Alikavazovic (translated by Daniel Levin Becker); *Like Hearts Swelling*, Polmo Polpo; *Love and Living*, Thomas Merton; *Love's Work*, Gillian Rose; *Music for Spaceships and Forests*, Twi the Humble Feather; *On Being Blue*, William Gass; *Run Towards the Danger*, Sarah Polley; *Sleepless Nights*, Elizabeth Hardwick; *Slow Focus*, Fuck Buttons; *Splinters*, Leslie Jamison; *Tonight I'm Someone Else*, Chelsea Hodson; *The Undiscovered Self*, Carl Jung; *The Undying*, Anne Boyer; *Un Verano Sin Ti*, Bad Bunny; *We've Been Going About This All Wrong*, Sharon Van Etten.

CREDITS

EDITORIAL
Eric Chinski
Jackson Howard
Brianna Fairman

REPRESENTATION AND RIGHTS
Jin Auh
Abram Scharf
Anna Haddelsey
Jessica Bullock
The Wylie Agency

TEXT DESIGN
Gretchen Achilles

JACKET DESIGN
Alex Merto

PRODUCTION MANAGER
Nina Frieman

PRODUCTION EDITORS
Carrie Hsieh
Nancy Elgin

MANAGING EDITORS
Debra Helfand
Scott Auerbach

PUBLICITY
Brian Gittis

MARKETING
Daniel del Valle
Hillary Tisman
Nicholas Stewart
Caitlin Cataffo
Sam Glatt
Jonathan Woollen
Isabella Miranda

CONTRACTS
Erika Seidman
Penny Chu

SALES
Spenser Lee

COPYEDITING
Nancy Clements

PROOFREADING
NaNá V. Stoelzle
Susan Bishansky

Praise for *The Möbius Book*

"This wry, surprising, nimble book—allergic to genre labels, and positively vibrating with insight—achieves what only great art can manage: to be both impossible to imagine, and utterly necessary. I was absolutely spellbound."
—Leslie Jamison, author of *Splinters*

"A singular, bewitching work about cycles of life and loss, the patterns of behavior that seem to lock us into who we are, and the quest for a faith that might break us free."
—Hua Hsu, author of *Stay True*

"A brilliantly innovative memoir-cum-novel that unsettles and enthralls. As Catherine Lacey navigates a winding path of loss and self-discovery, she meditates on spirituality, the illusion of safety, the nature of art, and the transformative power of rupture; the result is a meditation of startling immediacy and depth."
—Meghan O'Rourke, author of *The Invisible Kingdom*

THE MÖBIUS BOOK

THE MÖBIUS BOOK

CATHERINE LACEY

FARRAR, STRAUS AND GIROUX • NEW YORK

Farrar, Straus and Giroux
120 Broadway, New York 10271

Copyright © 2025 by Catherine Lacey
All rights reserved
Printed in the United States of America
First edition, 2025

Title-page art by Foto-Ruhrgebiet / Shutterstock.com.

Library of Congress Cataloging-in-Publication Data
Names: Lacey, Catherine, 1985– author.
Title: The Möbius book / Catherine Lacey.
Description: First edition. | New York : Farrar, Straus and
Giroux, 2025. Bound together back-to-back and inverted
(tête-bêche), each with its own title page.
Identifiers: LCCN 2024053381 | ISBN 9780374615406 (hardcover)
Subjects: LCSH: Lacey, Catherine, 1985– | LCGFT: Fiction. |
Creative nonfiction.
Classification: LCC PS3612.A335 M63 2025 | DDC 813/.6—
dc23/eng/20250131
LC record available at https://lccn.loc.gov/2024053381

Designed by Gretchen Achilles

Our books may be purchased in bulk for promotional,
educational, or business use. Please contact your local bookseller
or the Macmillan Corporate and Premium Sales Department at
1-800-221-7945, extension 5442, or by email at
MacmillanSpecialMarkets@macmillan.com.

www.fsgbooks.com
Follow us on social media at @fsgbooks

1   3   5   7   9   10   8   6   4   2

For Sean, Sara, and Wilhelmina

THE MÖBIUS BOOK

E die's on the line, says she's coming over, says it's urgent, no context.

Of course, Marie says, *but where are you now? Where have you been?* Dial tone. Marie returns the receiver to its cradle, turns off the ringer for the night. A landline. How quaint. When she goes out, nobody can reach her.

Two locks and a dead bolt, closing the door, locking all three behind her. Everyone here lives like this, though they smile and say hello to each other in the hallways. Marie, too, smiles and says hello—but you can't trust anyone who would chose to live here, such a place between places.

Down four flights, out the front door, down the block to the corner, to one of the very last pay phones in the city. The pay phone had been one of the main reasons she'd chosen this bleak and liminal neighborhood over the other bleak and liminal neighborhoods she could afford. Proximity to something so irrevocably stuck in the past.

Was she going to go through with it this time? And if she did call, what would she say? Marie had done this before, braced herself to stand within the phone booth's urine-y air as she considered breaking the no-contact streak by calling K. Like the way a smoke break broke up the workday, walking out to the pay phone to maybe but never actually make that call had a way of breaking up her life into discrete pieces, a constant loop of considering and concluding.

But again she leaves the phone booth, walks the half-block home, passes through the building's lock gauntlet, skips the elevator for the stairwell, ascends to the fifth floor, and she would have gone directly to her apartment door, she would have gone directly there without stopping, every step evenly paced to follow the last, she would have done that if she hadn't noticed a puddle of what seemed to be blood seeping beneath her neighbor's door.

She stops, looks at it. Blood. It could be nothing else. The body recognizes its filling with no effort. A smell. A heavy sheen. Maybe even a low frequency sound picked up by her body hair.

Still staring at the blood, Marie listens for the voices of the man and woman who live behind that door, voices she hears often through their shared wall, though she doesn't know their faces. In the six months since moving in she has avoided crossing paths with them.

But as she listens for their voices now, with the blood there, shining, the puddle perhaps still expanding, all she hears is air rapidly entering and exiting her body; then, without quite realizing it, she is back in her apartment, locking the two locks, the dead bolt. She is still standing at the door, unaware of how much time has passed. Already she is considering returning to the hot, yellow air of the pay-phone booth, and maybe, this time, she'll make the call.

But if she went out again she would have to pass by that door, and the blood might have expanded out into the hallway to the extent that she would be left with no choice but to jump over it, and possibly by the time she returned after visiting the pay phone the blood could have expanded even further, widening to the point at which she could not even jump over it without the risk of a splatter. So, no. She isn't going out again. She sits on the concrete floor by the large, dirty window facing that little plaza between two factories where she often sees the same people, daily, on their lunch breaks. But it's Saturday and dark already and all she sees are two men, side by side on a bench, both wearing hats despite the unseasonable heat, both with their arms folded across their chests.

The doorbell rings and now Marie is back in this life, remembering the blood next door, remembering the blood in her own body, remembering Edie's coming over. *Where's Edie?*

Through the squint at the center of the door—Edie. Edie
and nothing but a kind of guilty smile and a duffel bag. Marie
opens the door and takes Edie in her arms, peering out
quickly to reconfirm that, yes, there is a small but obvious
puddle of dark liquid at the neighboring apartment's door,
but when she releases Edie and sees her unbothered face, she
decides not to ask if she saw it, too. It's been too long, and
she doesn't want to begin the night with the possibility of a
murder next door.

Where have you been?

Edie doesn't answer, slips past Marie and into the bathroom—
I'll explain—and shuts the door behind her.

Like a mirage, the way a road up ahead on a hot day can
seem wet and shimmering. *Maybe there's some kind of heat
in my head,* she thinks, *some kind of heat in my life that's
distorting things.* A waking dream. A dreamy fear. It's a
theory.

The bathroom door opens, and Edie is standing there with
water dripping off her face, her hands. There's black makeup
smeared under her eyes.

Towel?

Under the sink.

Edie buries her face in a white towel, then looks down at the black streaks she's left.

Doesn't matter, Marie says, but Edie starts soaping it and scrubbing it out in the sink. *Doesn't matter*, she says again, but Edie keeps at it.

Everyone says you're having a crisis, Marie says, standing in the bathroom doorway, speaking to Edie in the mirror.

Who's everyone?

No one, just me . . . no one.

Edie keeps scratching the stain from the washcloth.

And anyway, how could I be having a crisis when I'm obviously so happy? Edie smiles. *This isn't even fake*, she says, all her teeth visible. *This is a genuine smile.*

It's fine—we don't have to talk about it.

The little towel, wet and white again, on the sink's lip. She stares at it. The lips of things—for the life of Edie—why did they stir such odd pity?

And actually everyone says that you're the one having the crisis.

Because it's true. I am, walking away as Edie follows. *I am having a crisis. But I'm also having tea, do you want some?*

Marie opens her cupboard where a cluster of teacups huddle on a shelf too small to contain them. She picks the light blue one, the one she's partial to, crude and mass produced, saved from a stoop in a rich person's neighborhood, one of those piles of abandoned objects that couldn't live up to the lives of their owners. Almost everything in Marie's apartment has been defined by such rejection.

Marie's setting a kettle to boil when Edie reaches for a cup and knocks it to the floor and into pieces. *Doesn't matter,* Marie says from the kitchen, not even checking to see what broke. But Edie is already rummaging in the junk drawer for the superglue she left when she helped Marie move into this place on an awful, late-summer day.

Broken things matter, Edie says, and Marie can't help but blurt back, *You don't have to get philosophical about everything that happens to you. Not everything's a sign—*

Are you OK? Edie cuts in.

What?

Is there something wrong?

Of course there is, Marie says, thinking, *Blood Blood Blood.*

And that ends it. Edie's eyes well up and Marie goes to hold her, softly first then firmer and firmer until whatever it is has passed. This is why people know each other. Soon, everything is more or less restored, and the kettle whistles, and Marie takes it off the heat while Edie collects the shards. In silence, they make a truce because each of them needs the other on this night more than they are able to admit. A special kind of disdain can grow out of this sort of need if one isn't careful.

They hold tea too hot to drink and sit in the heavily weathered furniture, waiting to know what to say and how to say it.

You've left him for good this time? Marie asks.

Almost three months now.

A season.

Merry Christmas, by the way.

And where did you go at first?

I was staying with K. I knew they had room, so . . .

Oh.

Are you mad?

How is K?

You're not mad?

Of course not, but is—

You don't want to know.

Sure. I don't. But I would, obviously—and it seems like a stupid question—but I'd like to know how you are.

Edie doesn't scream. Edie doesn't slide out of her chair to get a laugh, nor does she ride an imaginary horse into the sunset, and she doesn't mime shooting herself in the head, slitting her own throat, or dragging her body across the floor toward the window to beg the moon for mercy. Edie does none of these things, but Marie can sense it all when Edie shrugs and stutters—*O-oh, you know.*

Marie is thinking of the day, five or six years back, when Edie came over to say that she'd met some guy and everything was different now and she had to go, had to go at once—*It's the only way, the only reasonable way,* she kept repeating—a slight smile but a kind of death in the eyes, a resignation, something in her that had been given over; the part of Edie that always found smaller and smaller corners to wedge herself into was so alive.

Marie had recognized this look in Edie's face with the same part of herself that so often returned, instinctually, to the

familiar scenes and types of people she best knew. And though there are things she could say to Edie now, there was nothing to say to Edie on that day all those years ago, nothing anyone could say or do to a woman with that much faith in the fire she was happily setting.

Both Marie and Edie's compulsion toward the past was chronic, and this compulsion toward the past was also a compulsion toward the familiar, and their compulsion toward the familiar had an ungodly velocity and was openly hostile toward their various other compulsions, desires, even basic needs. Their compulsion toward the familiar was most powerful in the fact that neither of them realized she had it. This compulsion was, above all, extremely ordinary.

Edie had said she was moving into his cabin in the wilderness, seven hours down five different highways, and she was going immediately—*it's the only option, really*—and the fact that she hardly knew this man, and that she was fleeing from another man she'd once fled toward years ago with a similar intensity, dropping the things she'd once wanted and suddenly wanting all that he wanted, a man she'd fled toward when fleeing yet another man, same chorus, different verse, same Edie, different year, same cycle, different black hole to throw herself into, and it was obvious to everyone except Edie that this was the worst case yet, though it was also true that she had to get down to the bottom of the well, that there could be no other way for her to break out of this pattern unless it broke her first.

It's like she's advanced to the highest level of a video game, Marie thought as Edie calmly reported her plans that day to move, immediately, because he was living a better, more real, more honest way of life than she was, and they were in love in a way that necessitated drastic choices, and Edie knew—she knew—it would be enough. Already Marie could hear his voice in hers, his logic in her friend's soft mouth.

We're going to beat this thing for good, Edie had said, though Marie could tell from the pride in Edie's voice that she was repeating something the new guy had told her, so she didn't ask why she was describing love as something that needed to be conquered.

The twins had just been born and Marie's wife was nursing one of them in the corner of the living room, grimacing as she tried to treat the constant breaking and bleeding and scabbing on the other breast. No one had slept normally in their home for several weeks or months, and an absent urgency had taken over their every movement; all their decisions came to them out of the engine of instinct and never a fully conscious thought, and in a way Edie was in a similar place between places, all instinct, no thinking.

Yes, she'd said to Edie all those years ago now, *I understand. There's no other way.* But Marie was thinking only of a classic Nintendo-style Edie jumping from crumbling rock to crumbling rock, climbing a 2D mountain to fight the final monster of the game. *Except she has no idea*, Marie thought, *she has*

no idea what sort of level she's reached. And there it was, that honeyed disdain that can develop between two people who know each other intimately yet still fall short of telling the most intimate truths.

Busy, busy, busy Edie seemed to be, working so hard, day and night it sometimes seemed, using both hands, at all times, working tirelessly to make her life more difficult than it had to be.

It's just that—Edie is struggling to find the right words—*it's natural to want to spend your years with someone, but I keep ending up in these dreadful situations.*

Dreadful! What a word!

Dreadful, Edie says again, trotting the word out again as if to humiliate it. *But it was.* Her eyes glass over as she smiles.

It's not your fault that it was—

You don't know that.

Maybe I don't, but I do. I know what kind of man he is.

Marie leaves that phrase there, hoping Edie will confirm it, finally, will tell her what happened, will tell her things that Marie can intuit but can't know for sure. Edie won't tell her. Edie won't tell anyone for months or years or maybe ever.

Instead, Edie will say things like, *I know I can be very difficult to live with*, or Edie will say, *I was so selfish, I was so selfish and I never thought of him, never took care of him*, or she'll say, *I must have ruined it, that's the kind of person I am.* Edie won't tell Marie tonight about the time he threw a book across the room at her, about how it momentarily woke her up and she almost left until he talked her back down into believing it was her fault, that she had to be better, that she had to be more honest with him, more attentive, more giving. She was overreacting, anyway. It was just a book. His shock at her shock! Nothing was going to hurt her. It was all in her head, her damaged little head that only he could see clearly and understand and still love.

It obviously wasn't going to hit you
    But how did I know if it—
I knew
    But I didn't know
Even if it did hit you, you would have been fine
    I'm already not fine
You're fine
    I'm not
You're making a huge deal out of nothing
    But you threw a book at me
You were being crazy You're still being crazy
    I don't see why that has anything to do with
You don't have to be crazy.
You're acting like a child.
You act like a child because you are *a child.*

And it was true that Edie was acting like a child. Often, around him, she had felt like a child. More often than not this had been a good thing, hadn't it? Seeing the world as a child does. Having the energy of a child. Playing with their dog as a child would, laughing, sometimes unable to stop laughing, awed, so often awed over ordinary things. Trusting him to make all their decisions, to know what's best, to explain the world to her. Being disinterested in the murk and mire of adulthood—money, the future, insurances, appearances. The way she had, at eight, not given a damn about whether her clothes were dirty or whether her hair was combed. It was beautiful (*wasn't it?*) this reprise of girlhood in her thirties. But a child's love is an obedient love, and that night had opened up the possibility of not obeying.

Then there was another night, another story Edie won't ever tell Marie or K or anyone, the night he'd pounded a wall with two fists in the middle of a lecture to her about how insulting her tone of voice had been, and the bookcase had trembled and a heavy bookend had toppled over, hit Edie in the face, given her a bloody nose.

She stood there, shocked, arms outstretched for some reason, as blood drops came down to the floor.

Tilt your head back, he'd said with the exact intimate tone her father had used when she'd gotten a bloody nose on his watch as a kid, and later she found out that tilting backward is the exact wrong thing to do for a bleeding nose, but she

did as she was told, both as a girl and right then, and tasted blood in the back of her throat; but when he'd come toward her with a dish towel, she'd instinctively flinched away from his hand, and he threw the towel at her feet. *You're trying to make me seem like a villain! This is not my fault!*

Not his fault, not his fault, not his fault. And she did feel bad. It's true he never really hit her, or at least he never hit her in the way that people mean when they say *My husband used to hit me,* or *I saw my father hit my mother sometimes,* or when they ask, gently, *Did he hit you?* It wasn't like that, was it? No. So Edie was just making it worse when she anticipated that kind of violence from his anger. She was just making it worse. She always was making it worse.

Well, what kind of man was he, Edie asks Marie, genuinely curious, *if you say you know.*

You know.

OK. Maybe. It was just, you know, an intense few years. He feels so much.

Marie can't say anything to this, how sad it is to hear that Edie can't stop trying to explain his every action, how impossible for her to see him as simply responsible for himself. No, someone or something else was always responsible for his actions—his past, how unfair it had been, his migraines, his

heart condition, his grief—though usually it had been Edie, Edie who had been responsible for making him angry, for provoking it out of him. She sometimes had the feeling she was something he had saved and therefore owned.

Marie knows that harming someone is one of the fastest ways to become permanent in them. How terrible. The worst days are so tended to, visited and revisited in memory, put on an altar with the harshest lighting.

In an effort to counteract this, Marie never spoke about any-one who'd ever harmed her, and it disgusted Marie when she thought of the possibility that she'd become permanent in her wife in this exact way. But of course she had. She knew she had. She'd done something to the woman she loved for which she feared she could never sufficiently apologize.

Did you have any contact with him after you left?

He had to go through K, Edie says.

How?

If there was anything he wanted to say to me, he had to tell it to K, then K would tell it to me.

It was easy for Marie to imagine K taking on this responsibil-ity, handling these communications like someone from the

army hidden in a hazmat suit. K had always fallen naturally into roles of authority, though they also claimed to detest hierarchies of any kind. Their comfort in exerting control was one of the reasons K had set up Marie with their sister, introducing them with a heavy push—*I know everything about Marie, about both of you really, everything, and she's perfect for you, you're perfect for each other.* Marie, knowing K did not know everything about her, not even close, smiled at K's sister anyway, and felt a little sick sliding into the diner booth beside a woman she already knew, on instinct, she would someday marry—a rite she'd never previously expected herself capable of enacting—an instinct quickly countered by her belief that all marriages either ended in sudden disaster or festered slowly for years, then ended in sudden disaster, and so as Marie felt her thigh pressed against this woman's thigh and as she looked at this familiar face—the feminine version of K's face—she knew on a visceral, unreachable, nauseating level that she would love this woman more than she would love anyone, and at the same time she knew she was bound to lose her someday, bound to be destroyed by that loss, bound to hurtle toward it anyway, unable to outrun entropy. K's awful boyfriend that summer, a pretty blond from a rich family, was laughing at the two of them from across the diner booth, Marie and K's sister visiting from out of town, Marie and the woman she would marry, Marie and the woman who would leave her—*ooooh, look at you two. Who's gonna drive the U-Haul? Ha ha ha.* Where on earth did K keep finding these awful, gorgeous jerks?

Edie's first real smile of the night is on her face now as she begins to tell Marie the story of one of the last times he tried to reach her, through K, three weeks after she'd left.

Tell her I have been thinking a lot about how things went, the text read, *and I need to talk to her.*

K put down the phone and repeated it to Edie: *He's been thinking about things and he wants to talk to you.*

He's been thinking about things? That's really what he said?

K read directly from the screen: *"Tell her I have been thinking a lot about how things went and I need to talk to her."*

In K's voice the message was defanged and could be studied. He was using that stock phrase a person uses when they're trying to make amends, when they're trying to insinuate guilt without making an actual admission. But Edie knew that he never apologized and he never used stock phrases. These were two of his credos, two forms of his particular power: his constant lack of apology and his ongoing attempt to never resemble, however briefly, anyone else.

So he was, Edie knew, using this language quite on purpose, a tactic to get her on the phone, to get her full attention, to prepare her for an apology and give her something else. To exert his power once more.

I am not coming to the phone, Edie said to K, who typed the message back to this man until the screen lit up—*It's him, he's calling.*

K answered and Edie went outside and walked toward a tree in the yard as if she had something she needed to tell it. The man on the phone tried to persuade K to reframe his request to speak to Edie in a way that he thought might convince her to come to speak to him, to give him a chance to explain himself, but when that failed for long enough that K told him, *I'm hanging up now*, he asked K to ask Edie if she would give her consent to allow him to dedicate his next book of photography, a series of self-portraits, to her.

K, leaning out the side door, shouted this proposal at Edie, who was crouched to study the acorns and dirt and pebbles.

He wants to know if he can dedicate his self-portrait book to you!

Edie walked slowly toward the house, unsure of how she'd respond until she spoke.

Tell him . . . it is extremely clear . . . to whom his self-portraits are actually dedicated.

K returned to the phone and sanitized it: *Edie feels the dedication is of no consequence.*

Marie is laughing as if she were there, too—*of all the thousands of photos he's taken, it's the selfies that are dedicated to you*—laughing just as she used to laugh with K, a loss that undercuts Marie's laughter but not enough to end it, and Edie is laughing, too—*It's the only time I ever had just the right thing to say at just the right moment, I never do*—then Edie stops laughing before Marie does.

You've always loved difficult things, Marie says, deep breath now, talking about Edie but just as well talking about herself. *Like boxing—remember? You were sprained and bruised all the time, and you kept going.* She stops herself before saying: *I've never known anyone to love being brutalized as much as you.*

Edie's eyes light up—*Is that a crowbar?*

It is. It was in the closet when Marie moved in, and now it's still the only work of art she's hung up, if it counts as that. She'd perched the crowbar on two big nails in the wall that had also been left behind by whomever had been here before her. Like a lover's ex, you know the previous tenant by her absence, the things abandoned, the shadows of habits she may have once had.

Edie takes it off the wall and holds it like a bat, ready to swing.

Is this the kind of place you need a crowbar?

Someone thought so.

Well it was nice of them to leave it for you.

Maybe, Marie says, thinking of the blood, then not thinking of blood, thinking of it, then not again, quickly like that, like a tremble, then it's gone.

You know what I think, Edie says as she hangs the crowbar back up, *I think people who say they're happy in their relationship either haven't gotten to the real relationship yet, or they're lying.*

So you've become a fatalist that fast?

I hope not.

Sounds like it.

It's a theory.

You told us all the time that you were happy, that it was a good relationship. Were you lying to yourself or to us?

No—I was happy. That's the fucked-up thing. It was so predictable, there were all these limits.

It felt safe?

In a way. Extremely dangerous and extremely safe at once.

Do you ever feel like worrying about this stuff is just frivolous, that Holzer was right that romantic love is just a lie invented to control women?

It's true that it often does seem to control people. But that doesn't mean it's a lie. Just that it has power.

Power over women.

Over men, too. So, no, I guess I don't agree entirely. There's some truth to it, but I don't think it's true.

You don't want it to be true.

You know—I almost do want it to be true. The permission to just fuck around and live alone forever and never need anyone else's company in particular, and for that never to seem lacking. But maybe it's the fact that the body decays that makes this kind of intimacy important.

So that someone finds you if you have a stroke? So that someone's there to clean up your vomit after the chemo?

Yeah, I guess so.

But if that's the role, then it seems like the selection process is asking all the wrong questions. Or it's like—people fall in love for reasons that are nice at the time and totally useless a year later.

Neither of them speaks for a minute. Marie is wondering if her wife said yes to her proposal for all the wrong reasons. Marie could so easily make her laugh, for instance. She could always make her wife laugh. How many couples who are fundamentally incompatible together got married simply because one could make the other laugh? How many billions in lawyer fees were paid by women divorcing people they had married because of all that easy laughter? And Marie could still hear her wife's, her ex-wife's, laughter. Sometimes it seemed she could hear nothing else, and for a moment Marie is terrified by the prospect that Edie has really come here to stay up all night talking about love and relationships and how they go wrong. *How many days is she planning to stay? How many hours can I last like this?*

If there were right questions, Edie says, breaking Marie's introspection, *I wouldn't know what they are. The pilot's drunk.*

What?

Whatever—it is—that is—in charge of this? This, me thing? Whatever is up there pressing the controls—she's drunk. I have to wait for her to sober up.

You mean—you? You're drunk?

This is chamomile! I'm fine. I just mean I made the choice to give up my autonomy to him, to trade it for what felt like protection, or

deliverance—after how many gender studies classes? How stupid am I?

Well, you skipped class a lot.

Anyway, I always thought it would be K or you who'd take care of me if I was really sick.

Not him?

It always seemed like he'd be dead before I needed care. He talked about it so frequently, I sometimes felt like he was, in fact, dying right then. Thinking he was going to die at any moment, I mean—it narrowed my focus.

On him?

Always.

Edie and Marie are silent again, running over, out of order, and with much distortion, the evidence in their lives that a romantic love persisting through the years was achievable, and the evidence of its inevitable and excruciating decline. Faith in the costs. Fear of the costs.

Then Edie crawls onto the ground, lies face down, and says, *In love you place your life in another's hands, and you dare them to ruin it.*

There you go again with your brooding one-liners.

It was a romantic notion, though a stupid one, and it reminded Marie of how song lyrics have a way of seeming true—how almost anything can seem true when set to music or rhyme, no matter how inane, no matter how mind-numbing and reductive and even destructive these notions could be. Sometimes Marie suspected that Edie—as adventurous and considerate as she was—had also readily accepted nearly every stupid, seductive idea that had ever found her, which meant her life was a continual attempt to disentangle herself from all these beloved falsehoods, but all she ever did was further ensnare herself in every mental trap within reach.

I really have never been happier than now, alone, Edie says, still lying on the floor. She rolls on her back. *Though, maybe happiness is the wrong measurement, in the question about happy relationships, I mean—I think it's worse than that. I think most of those people are not even doing well. I think they're held together by a dozen lies mortared together with blindness.*

Marie cannot listen to Edie's overblown metaphors for another moment, she thinks, tired as she is of dwelling on the black hole of the end of love, the fallibility of the human heart, and, by extension, divorce in general, and Marie's own divorce in specific, and the fact of the twins, and the matter of custody, the behaviors that qualified or disqualified a person from taking care of a child, the issues of maternity, and the fact that her ex-wife had given actual birth to the twins, the

fact that Marie had always joked that she wanted (ha ha) to be a father anyway—to have the ha ha emotional detachment of the father, the ha ha learned helplessness of the father, the ha ha staunchly protected privacy of the father—and all of this had led her to the looming truth of her inevitable lack of consequence or claim in the lives of those four people who had once constituted the entirety of her days: the twins, her estranged wife, and K.

Though Marie had once been the legal co-parent (and genetic nonparent) of the twins, now the children she had once called *her* children were more related to K, Marie's ex–sibling-in-law and ex–best friend, the person who had caused both the onset and the downfall of her marriage, and Marie is *tired*, so tired of it, so she gets out the mezcal and two caballitos and places them on the coffee table rigged from milk crates and plywood. She sets the mezcal and tiny glasses down delicately, service for holy water.

Sitting up and seeing it, Edie knows she's being a pain, and this was Marie's solution to numb it. Two shots poured. Two shots taken. Then Marie, in silence, walks to the part of the room that serves as the kitchen to make two peanut butter and jelly sandwiches, cutting the crusts off as a joke to Edie, or cutting the crusts off because the twins always asked for it that way, or cutting the crusts off because for a minute she doesn't remember where she is, this grim warehouse apartment where she moved when she had to, when she came home from work to find all her clothes and books piled in her

front yard, her wife in such a wide-eyed panic all she could do was whisper in a strained monotone—*you fucking monster, did you think no one was ever going to find out, how long have you been lying, K told me what they saw, are you crazy, are you actually crazy, don't answer that*—while the twins slept. *You better be gone by the time they wake up. I don't care where you go. No one cares where you go.*

Marie sets a plate of crustless, white sandwiches in front of Edie and says, *Ha ha, I'm a good father, ha ha,* but Edie doesn't look up.

Marie is still standing, holding her plate and chewing and staring at nothing as she runs through her theories of what—the possibility of a hallucination set aside for now—may or may not have happened in her neighbor's apartment. If it was true that Marie had seen a wet and expanding puddle of something seeping from under their door, and if that puddle was indeed a puddle of blood, and if that blood could be traced back to a human body instead of some more medical and maybe less human container, then this would indicate that someone had either been murdered, had an accident, or taken or tried to take their own life in the neighboring apartment. All three possibilities were the sorts of things you might expect to happen in a building such as this one, a place where the light bulbs in the hallway were sometimes stolen, a place where indescribable sounds could be heard in the night, odd wails and unidentifiable machinery churning.

Marie is finishing her sandwich now, unaware of how mechanically she was eating as she thinks over the likelihood that a dead or dying body is next door, bleeding out, and if the blood was the result of a successful or attempted murder, then the person who had stabbed or otherwise punctured the bleeding body would, it seems, still most likely be inside the apartment, given the undisturbed nature of the puddle of blood blocking the one and only means of egress of the apartment, which would mean that this person or people who had stabbed the bleeding body were likely still in the apartment, which would mean that on the other side of the wall where the crowbar was hanging was a person or people with a knife or similar instrument who could be, it seems, quite capable of using it.

Marie is trying not to think of any of this—*there's nothing I can do, nothing to be done, it's not my problem*—while Edie keeps staring at her, grinning as she waits for Marie to notice.

Man, you are fucking spaced out . . .

What?

Are you OK?

Hey, did you see anything coming out from under the neighbor's door?

The what?

The apartment next door. Did you see a puddle of something by their door?

Actually, yeah, I was going to ask but I had to pee so bad I forgot. Paint or something?

Oh, right, probably just paint. They're—I think they're artists. The people that live there.

And with this, Marie cauterizes her nerves—not blood, just paint, no death, just mess—and Edie starts talking about her sex life, how she had never been more fearless than she is now, and she'd even picked up some guy in the middle of the day in a park, the animal immediacy of it, how it forced a person out of her head and into the—

That's great, Edie, Marie says, but her tone betrays her lack of interest, and Edie rolls her eyes—

I know you think that the only way to have good sex is for it to be a secret until you get caught.

Cheap shot.

Sorry, but it's true.

Needing to apologize for a somewhat true-ish but unnecessarily brutal statement is practically the definition of a cheap shot.

Fine.

You were telling me about your sex life—the men in parks or whatever—please, go on.

And Edie does go on talking about how reborn she feels, *that's the actual word she's using,* Marie thinks, *reborn,* such an irritating choice, to describe her unhindered libido as a period of rebirth, or maybe it is simply and unfortunately true that Edie has always tended to describe her life in religious terms—religious as she is, though lacking a religion—yet it is also true that Edie has never seemed happier, and it's true that Marie loves Edie, and loves to see her happy even on these dubious grounds. Fucking without context or remorse—is this maturity or its identical twin, compartmentalization?

At times, the length of Edie and Marie's friendship, a full half of their lives—the entirety, so far, of both of their adulthoods—at times it felt that knowing someone this intimately and for such a critical duration had been and may continue to be the main event of Marie's life. Being in love and later being married had been more urgent, more time-consuming, and in some ways more intimate, but nothing had felt more central and reliable than the conversation that had been happening between the two of them, and, at least until recently, with K. This long witnessing, on even ground— unlike the angled perspective between parent and child or the concave mirror of marriage—had created an unwritten

record within each of them about how the other had or had not changed, an archive of actions and habits that became more detailed and more critical with every passing year.

Marie had met K and Edie when she was seventeen, just shy of eighteen, gawkish and awkward and closeted, freshman year, still a child in her newly adult body. K and Edie, who'd spent their whole childhoods together, adopted her into their friendship as if they'd been looking for her all this time, and many years ago, though Marie could hardly stand to recall this now, K had told her that she, on her twenty-fourth birthday, was *so easy to love*, a statement she would have been unable to accept from anyone else, not from a girlfriend, not from her own family, and when K's sister used this exact phrase in her vows to Marie on their wedding day, unaware of what it echoed, Marie had blushed. She knew it was a lie.

As a girlfriend she hadn't been easy to love, and as a wife she knew she still wouldn't be easy to love. Marie was melancholic, indecisive, and anxious. She had insomnia so strong it was often contagious, and when she did sleep she hogged the blankets. She couldn't cook, barely cleaned, and had a regular habit of getting drawn into long conversations with neighbors and colleagues when she should have been on her way home for dinner or carrying out an errand she promised she'd do or meeting her wife somewhere on the rare nights they went out. Above all she knew she wanted too much from romantic love, held it to impossible standards, wanted it to totally redeem her, somehow, effortlessly and constantly. But

Marie did believe that she was good at friendship, easy in it, never asking anything unreasonable of the platonic, always relaxing into the human texture, the natural ebbing and flowing of her bonds with K and Edie. She gave herself up without tension into friendship, respected her friends enough to allow them to change her.

It was Edie who had, one day toward the end of their third year in college, said to Marie, *I think you're past it now.* And she didn't have to say more than that. Marie knew exactly what Edie meant, yet it was only in hearing Edie make this observation about this change that Marie suddenly knew and felt it to be true—that tenacious streak of self-hatred, that ambiguous but inescapable sense of being a failure, the stiffened way she'd been occupying her body—for years it had been lifting but had lifted almost entirely the moment that Edie said this—*I think you're past it now*—or at least the first layer of it had lifted, and Marie knew the only reason this change had been possible was the way she'd been absorbed into K and Edie's world—they, the pair of friends who'd come to college together, platonic prom dates, everyone said they'd be together in the end, those kind of friends. Even as children they knew they were already together in the end—it was already the end, and they were already together. K and Edie's relationship seemed to be the most radical and rare thing to Marie—a true marriage, a marriage without marriage—and for years she'd thought herself ancillary to the two of them, a role she felt at home in, an additional person, a spare, a friendly ghost, until it was clear, all at once in the August

she turned twenty-one, that she was, a shock to herself, no less essential, just a newer element, the obvious third point of the triangle.

The three of them had lived in a crooked and cheap little apartment for a time during and after college, the soft and uncomplicated years before jobs and partners and graduate school and travel had peeled them apart, and though each of those transitions had seemed final or potentially final, none had yet proven so. The moves to other cities or other apartments in the same city seemed to signal the end of an era and the likelihood that it would never be quite like this again, that they'd never live together again, that the nature of this family was once again changing. But relationships that had seemed permanent had ruptured, jobs were lost, new moves were needed, and graduations ended in nothing but a more advanced state of the confusion that had led to grad school in the first place, and it was then that one of them always returned to one or the other or both of them, hovering for a few weeks or months in a guest room, changing their lives once more with the assurance that their conversation and their jointly held archive and their shared support may actually be the most stable thing in their lives, and though other aspects of adulthood may peak or crash, this thing between the three of them would change shape but never reach a conclusion.

In fact, the possibility of a diminished potency in her relationships with K and Edie had been the only fear Marie could not even bring herself to confess to her wife in the months before

the arrival of the twins. All the other fears—the medical and mortal fears, the fears of their marriage getting filleted by two babies, the financial and logistical fears, the fear of failure—they had all seemed more dismissible than the worry she felt that she might lose her friends. It was clear that K and Edie were the axis of her life, though it seemed real adults were supposed to forge that kind of centrality elsewhere.

Marie's wife had always been certain that bearing and raising children was a central if not the sole purpose of her life, a certainty that was sometimes unsettling in its unquestioned steadiness, but Marie also knew her wife's certainty would be the lighthouse of their family life, the velocity that kept the whole thing aloft.

Then the twins came. They had been manageably unruly, without any major or lasting problems in their behavior or health or temperament, and Marie's transformation into a parent had not (as she had silently feared) ended her friendships with K or Edie, and it had even, in some ways, enriched them. Edie would occasionally obtain permission from her partner to visit Marie and the twins for a weekend, and she naturally became a child around the children, getting on the floor with them, inventing absurd games. When Edie looked up at Marie from the twins' angle, each saw new dimensions in the other.

Alone with the twins, noticing how intensely they surveilled Marie from their car seats and high chairs, how they

seemed to forget nothing and catalogued everything about their parents—words used in passing, momentary flickers of emotion, loose promises made then broken—Marie had often thought of and longed for the softer ways her friends had watched her, how different it was from the nonstop, existential intensity of those two little sets of eyes. Marie's wife did not, she knew, share this irritation at being watched so closely all the time, and it was possible, Marie thought, that her wife's innate impulse toward birth and child-raising had really been about this, all along—the desire to be witnessed with such life-or-death intensity, for her children to create hyperrealistic and micro-detailed portraits of their mother, and to live beneath them for the rest of their lives. Knowing this, knowing that these people who did not yet exist could be created and would in turn create this portrait of her—was this what Marie's wife envisioned as she walked with determination and authority into a sperm bank, mercilessly studied the options, and made her choice without hesitation?

During the years Marie had helped raise the twins, feeding them and ferrying them around and tucking them in and waking up with them once more, she felt that though there was so much humbling clarity in these daily acts, the one-directional devotion of parenting also felt a little demented and compulsive—similar to the way, at the height of her smoking, she'd sometimes realize she was inhaling from a cigarette she had no memory of lighting, like there was a ghost inside of her that smoked without her awareness—like

there was a ghost inside of her that went through the actions of parenting without her conscious participation. But she was good at it, she was told. Everyone said so.

Now that her marriage and relationship with the twins and her friendship with K had been severed in the course of a single afternoon, Marie's relationship with Edie was the most long-lasting thing in her life—Edie, Jesus, fucked up, feral, and precious as she is—and Marie is coming close to crying now, though she's smiling, watching Edie still talking about her exploits, remembering how Edie has always been able to give the best advice but never to take it, and how irritated Marie has always been by Edie's tendency to disappear for months on end, then show up as if she'd been there all along.

Marie is still watching her friend recount the details of some small orgy, distantly registering the facts of the event, but mainly she is just watching Edie's face, the wild gaze of someone newly introduced or reintroduced to the world. It's in that faint glimmer in her skin, in her eyes, her gestures, and of course her overblown word choice, her breathless way of speaking, the way she fidgets the fray on her shorts, curling her legs unnaturally in her chair, as if she isn't used to being alive, as if the life in her is constantly at risk of spilling out, rushing out everywhere and into everything.

Marie starts laughing and Edie says, *What?* and Marie says she doesn't know, that she's just out of it, but Edie asks again, *Out of what?*

Why are you telling me about all this?

Edie sits up, alert and formal as she recites an answer that seems rehearsed, how sexuality was one of the most beautiful and simple ways for a person to leave their mind and interact with the subconscious, or how sex was one of the few ways to exist directly as a body, as an animal, as a mortal and dying thing, and how sex also brought your awareness out of yourself and into the consciousness of another and how essential that was—but when Edie reaches the point in her response about the Paraclete, the soul, salvation, Marie pours another glass of mezcal and tilts it back quickly.

Good for Edie, really—good for her. But she had no self-awareness sometimes, and it was true that what Edie had been through was terrible, and it was true that it was good for her now to be finding pleasure in something, regardless of how frivolous, but Edie's recently past problems and their subsequent solutions all seemed so small right now, while Marie's problems were ongoing, they were serious and inescapable and quite frankly they were tragic, and perhaps the most tragic problem was that she could no longer have a reasonable relationship with the twins, and maybe even worse than that she was beginning to feel that the twins were never really hers in the first place, as they had never been genetically hers—the product only of her wife's body and the anonymous substance from the sperm bank—and though the genetics of the twins had never seemed consequential in the years she had lived with and raised them, her lack of genetic claim and her lack of do-

mestic responsibility now amounted to the fact that though she'd once had children, she now no longer had children, and perhaps they didn't even miss her, didn't need her, that she had perhaps always been something like a nanny in their life, removable, extraneous, easy to send away. It had become difficult to even say the word "my" before the word "children." *The twins.* It had come to that.

But is it true? Edie asks.

Is what true?

What K saw. That you were seeing someone else.

Seeing is a weird word for it, isn't it? Seeing—I can see you right now. I've seen a lot of people.

You know what I mean.

I do know what you mean. It just happens not to be a particularly simple situation, and no one knows that because no one asked me anything. K didn't ask me anything. My wife didn't ask me anything. You didn't even call.

I was out of town when it happened.

And where were you?

Greece. After I left him. For a month.

You went to Greece for a month?

Brenda was house-sitting and tickets were cheap.

So you went to Greece for a month. Great.

What's that supposed to mean?

It's just that—you're the sort of person that goes to Greece for a month, and I'm the kind of person who lives here.

Will you just tell me what happened?

But Marie doesn't know where to start, especially with someone who felt that sex with someone she barely even knew was or even could be something sacred when, in Marie's life, sex had mainly been something that brought people into her life or sent people out, the beginnings and endings of things.

How to tell it? She wants to tell Edie the truth, but she doesn't trust herself to know it.

It had seemed like a friendship at first, Marie says, but already she was getting things wrong. It hadn't seemed like a friendship; it had seemed, for reasons Marie could not completely discern, like a game, a series of challenges from this woman, Helena, a parent she'd met at day-care pickup years ago now, a mother with whom she'd exchanged num-

bers on the pretext that their kids might want to hang out, even though they could both tell that their kids didn't like each other, a fact made painfully clear on that one playdate a week later that ended with Helena's kid pushing one of the twins over and the other twin retaliating by taking a handful from the sandbox and forcing it into his mouth. *Next time, no kids*, Helena said, and Marie just felt her head nodding. *Anyway, this woman is married, and anyway, this woman is straight, and anyway, it's nothing*, and the next time they saw each other didn't happen until nine months later, a text from a name she'd nearly forgotten, a slow day at work anyway, an excuse to go downtown for lunch. That evening, when Marie's wife asked her how her day had been, Marie had simply not mentioned her lunch with Helena. She didn't tell her about how Helena had launched immediately into the most intimate conversation Marie had ever had with anyone she didn't actually, technically, know— Helena had been thinking about the nature of desire and power and men and women and how the reasons she had gotten married just ten years ago now already seemed so retro and regrettable, almost unmentionable, but she did believe in sticking it out, in sticking around even when it seemed doomed, when it seemed like she may never again feel *real sexual pleasure with another human body*, but then again, *What had even been the purpose of sexual pleasure in the first place?* she asked, undercutting the urgency with which she had just uttered the phrase "real sexual pleasure with another human body," and Helena claimed that she distrusted the urge toward sex, how it seemed that the people

who regularly followed that urge tended to be led around in circles, but still, lately she spent a lot of time thinking about how being in a couple seemed entirely at odds with being in a family and how it might be better if all the women just took all the children away from the men and raised them collectively, without the men, men who seemed only to get in the way, men who seemed so often to be no different than children, just larger. *Oh, but I don't really mean it, I do love my husband, what am I even saying, he's a good father, a great father,* she took a sip of wine, *I mean what am I even saying?* And Marie had tried to reassure her that this all seemed to be normal in a long marriage, the irritation at the edges of it, though Marie did not, at least not consciously, feel any of that irritation in her own long marriage. *It does seem like a lot to manage,* she said to Helena, an observation that seemed to calm Helena, a little, but Marie also noticed the tragic little tick in Helena's voice when she asked and rapidly answered two questions she'd pushed together into a single line: *But you're married right to a woman right?* Marie paused as if she needed to remember whether she was married (right?) to a woman (right?), then she said, as if reading the phrase, *Yes, I am.* The lunch went on, both of them increasingly tense, overly aware of their own breath and each other's every gesture, and at times Marie thought she was doing something wrong just by being there (though she couldn't identify what, exactly, was wrong with it), and at other times she thought she was being presumptuous to assume anything indecent about this lunch of salade niçoise and chenin blanc with Helena,

whose intentions, personal history, desires, middle name, fantasies, and current mental health status were all still to be, soon, discovered.

A month passed before they met again, a duration of time that made Marie feel that perhaps deciding not to mention the existence of this lunch with Helena to her wife (or even the existence of Helena) had been absolutely fine, as there was nothing to mention, and Marie accepted the spontaneous invitation for a coffee and a walk—*This morning? Now?*—thinking that she would, of course, tell her wife about Helena afterward, but the morning coffee spiraled into a long walk through a cemetery and a discussion of the purpose of sexual fantasy in general and the contents of their fantasies in specific, a conversation so frequently punctuated with *I can't believe I'm saying this* and *Why am I telling you this?* that shame itself was even worn away and nothing was taboo any longer. They touched only once that day—as they parted Marie had tried to use the vaguely formal contactless bow she'd gotten away with last time, but Helena went in for the European cheek-kiss and missed, landing on Marie's neck, wrecking Marie's composure for a fraction of a second, a fraction that Helena had recognized and taken in, and from that day onward their meetings became more frequent and passed with greater intensity, in stranger and stranger locations in order not to be observed, the secrecy of an affair but without any of the traditional forms of contact—without actual sex, for instance, without so much as a kiss. It was like a nineteenth-century courtship, but with conversations

that verged on the pornographic; brief, one-hour meetings and occasional phone calls during which they divulged secrets, asked questions that neither had ever asked anyone, and, eventually, each woman dared the other to fuck their spouses with special assignments—positions to use, words to say, and images to imagine. But they never touched each other—not like that—not physically, and because of that lack of contact Marie began to think of her time with Helena as time she was spending alone, or time she was doing something like therapy, or as time she was reading a book, a book called Helena, a book with whom she was on speaking terms. And maybe it could have gone on like that even much longer than their three years, with many extended breaks, which they each filled with remorse, swearing the whole thing off, laughing at it privately, then giving in again, sending a quick text, meeting up immediately to continue this erotic game. Then there was the day they each confessed that this was insane, it had been years, and all their discussions and dares and disclosures had to stop—*We aren't children*, Marie said, and though she wasn't entirely sure what she meant by that, Helena agreed, and from there they went straight to a hotel, texted lies about work to their spouses, and stayed in that hotel until it was time to go home and tuck their children into bed.

At which point we became reckless, Marie concluded to a placid-faced Edie, *and that's when K saw us, like a week later, making out in a hotel lobby where—*

The sound of several women screaming, and Edie and Marie are on their feet as if responding professionally, as if they'd each been sent to the same basic training: secure the premises, block the exits, locate the screaming women. Marie goes straight for the door and looks through the squint and is immediately mesmerized by the blood, the puddle of blood that has, it seems, expanded slightly—but then some laughter emerges from the screaming, and Edie says, *It's just some people in the street, they're fine, they're drunk.*

They're what? Marie turns sharply from the door, trying to forget the blood, *no it's paint—just a mess.*

Edie stands at the big window facing the street, looking out and down at a group of women getting out of a car, lighting cigarettes, shouting and laughing at each other in a way that sounded more pained than it really was. *They're probably neighbors of yours.*

Marie keeps staring at Edie, at the window, at reality, this is reality, your home is reality, next-door neighbors are not your reality, don't think of whatever it is, you can't do anything about whatever happened, stay here in your own home, with your own friend, her troubles, not the troubles of everything in the world, you can't do anything about it, someone died, maybe, someone was killed, maybe, but it's done with, the dead are not your concern, strangers are not your concern, you have to stay to see it through here with your own,

the woman in your home, the friend who needs you, the friend you need.

Edie wants to ask a thousand more questions about Helena, but resists, given the ghostly look in Marie's face.

You know, your story about the guy in the park reminded me of that trip I took to Oaxaca alone during college; didn't I tell you about it?

I can't remember, Edie says, relieved that Marie seems more relaxed now.

No—you remember, right? I was volunteering at the farm, and there was that hidden beach where the waves were too strong to even swim in—I've told you this.

If you told me . . . I guess I don't remember.

The fact that she'd either never told Edie or that Edie had forgotten this story felt impossible, yet one had to be true, but Marie immediately begins to tell or retell the story of the day she hiked alone to that beautiful hidden beach. She'd been fighting a bout of depression all that winter, and one of the only things that helped was going out to this isolated beach where she saw no one but animals, and she was lying there, listening to the ocean roar, when she realized that just on the other side of a small dune, partially visible when she turned her head, a man and a woman were completely

naked and fucking, and Marie, not wanting to interrupt what must have been such a nice time, turned her head the other way and pretended to be asleep though she couldn't help but hear, mixed with the howl of waves, each of them coming to climax, followed by their delirious laughter. Then she heard them get up and chase each other toward the water. Marie sat up then, and they noticed her and laughed even harder, waving at her, blowing kisses, then wading into the chaotic, churning water and splashing each other, washing the sand off their sweaty bodies; then the man slipped and was sucked out to sea, then hurled back in on a wave as he laughed and she laughed and even Marie laughed though it seemed profoundly dangerous, as there were signs in Spanish and English warning not to swim, that the ocean would win every time. But everything was OK—the lovers were laughing, the lovers kept surviving, splashing around in the water up to their knees, stopping to hold each other, to kiss with their wet arms wrapped around wet bodies.

It was so beautiful, so perfect, Marie says, starting to cry before she's even reached the tragic part of the story, the moment the man was sucked out again by the current but didn't come back, and his lover started shouting his name, then screaming it, then started swimming outward, and Marie heard a few more shouts, sharp and strange and far away, then nothing, then she ran past their wrinkled towels on the sand and through the woods, back to the farm, and told them they had to come quick though she knew it was too late, *Call the whatever you call, the coast guard, call them*, but there wasn't really

anyone to call, no one that could come quickly enough to go back in time.

I never told you this? Marie asked, tears on her motionless face.

How would I have forgotten it?

More laughter from the women in the street, and Marie goes to the window attempting to distance herself from the too-clear memory. She doesn't recognize them—young women in dresses and high heels and Santa Claus hats, lighting each other's cigarettes, singing carols off-key, their arms thrown around each other, young women having the time of their lives—but maybe one or some of them could live in the building.

Makes me want to smoke again, Marie says.

God I'm so glad you don't anymore. It's gross.

Marie fondly remembered the mesmerizing qualities of a cigarette, the magic trick of it, how it seemed capable of changing the direction of any given emotion. A woman she worked with that winter in Oaxaca had told her that she smoked to numb her anger, that everyone smoked to numb their anger, that was the whole point of smoking. *But be careful,* the woman had said, placing a hand on her throat, *you might need it someday.*

Mis pulmones? My lungs?

No, tu ira. Your anger.

Was this anger she felt now, now that she could no longer numb it? And to whom should she direct her anger? With what right could she access this anger?

You know it was K's idea that I come here, Edie says.

Why?

We didn't want you to be alone.

I've been alone for months.

It's Christmas.

What does that have to do with anything?

Do you want me to leave?

No.

Edie sits at the card table by the kitchen—two propane burners, a mini fridge, and a sink—and starts holding the pieces of teacup alongside each other, looking at the way it burst.

Marie goes to the front door, looks out the squint again.

Waiting on someone?

No. Just—wondering if . . . just looking.

Edie squeezes a little glue on one edge, then holds two shards hard against each other, re-creating the lost shape.

It's a kind of murder, isn't it? Edie asks, and it startles Marie—

It's—what? You think it is? Not an—accident or . . . ?

I mean you and K not speaking, you saying you're never speaking to K again, K saying they don't care. It's a kind of death. You're trying to murder each other out of your lives. And I'm the only witness.

It's the only thing that could, in that moment, really take Marie's attention away from the blood—the question of K, the question of whether they'll ever speak again, a question Marie had considered and solved several times over.

You think what K did is unforgivable—

Because it is.

You think that now but—

I'm not changing my mind.

What if K apologized?

Then they wouldn't be K.

What if they did?

What are you asking me, really? If K went against everything we know to be true about K and actually apologized to me, would I really be accepting that apology from K, seeing as K is completely unable to issue such an apology? The person K was is actually dead to me. That's the thing you don't want to acknowledge. That's the problem here. You can't—

So that's it? You never see K again?

Marie could feel her heart beating in her neck.

Yeah, Edie. That's it.

The anger throbs all over Marie's body just as it did the day she was scooping her things up from the yard, her wife locking all the doors in the house and texting her from behind the pulled blinds—*Go away. Never come back. Go away and never come back*—and so she called K, no answer, left an awful voicemail, received awful messages, sent awful messages. *Don't you even want to ask me what's going on, don't I deserve that?* and K telling her, *No. She's my sister. You betrayed my sister, so there's nothing to ask you.*

I just don't understand, Edie says, half the broken teacup in her hands, *why you two can't speak to each other. Just once. Twenty-three years.*

K had plenty of chances to speak to me, none taken. There are some things that just—you run out of time, you run out of time to do them.

But aren't you curious about what could happen? What K might say to you?

No.

You always told me that the reason you knew you'd never kill yourself was that you were curious enough about the future.

Suicide and never speaking to K are not the same thing, Edie.

To me, it's the same. To me it is. The two of you, the three of us—

I can't believe I have to say this, but this doesn't involve you and your monthlong trips to châteaus or whatever—

Can you—can you, be, just, a little less of an asshole right now?

A tense silence, then they're smiling. Marie sits across from Edie in one of the rusted folding chairs she found in an alley.

And they're not called châteaus in Greece, Edie says.

Marie watches in silence for a while as Edie keeps reassembling the broken teacup. Edie had always seemed to have dozens of other friends, none of them quite so conventional to be actually wealthy, but many of them clever enough to be wealth-adjacent, the sorts of young women who were often gifted the keys to summer homes and estates during the shoulder seasons. Years ago it often seemed that Edie was off in some glamorous place with friends Marie had never even heard of, and since the breakup it seemed this pattern had resumed. But Marie had never had or wanted a wide circle of friends. It was just K and Edie and sometimes one or two others, people who would float into her periphery for a few years, then drift out again. That Edie believes this rift between K and Marie was resolvable showed how Edie had no idea how serious the trespass had been.

I think it's a matter of faith, Marie says, as Edie stares at her, expressionless. *A relationship is an act of faith—it's a kind of magic or experiment, isn't it?* This is almost a real question. She's almost hoping Edie will answer with finality, with something simply true. *But it can be broken, like any faith, and it can't be restored. The problem was . . . when K did what they did, it became clear to me that the thing I had faith in, with K, it wasn't there. K didn't share that faith with me and I don't know how long it was gone, the other side of what I believed in.*

Even just the word—*"faith"*—bothers Edie, like the name of a parent who betrayed, then abandoned her, left her to fend for herself. At eighteen she still went to mass, still prayed,

still felt the presence of the Paraclete, but she did and felt this all in secret, even quietly hoped to join a convent, ever waiting to gain enough fortitude to devote herself entirely to Jesus, something she never told K or Marie, knowing neither of them wanted to understand or were even capable of understanding the lingering effect that all her childhood gnosis still had on her. They knew she'd been raised Catholic, and K still remembered when Edie was intense about it, witnessing to kids at school, going to Bible Club in the afternoons, but at some point Edie's Catholicism had slipped under the surface, becoming almost too intense for her to even mention—a hidden thing, more privately held than her own naked body.

But the semester she went to study in Athens—three courses in the classics—came at a time when her faith in the Nicene Creed was unraveling, as she felt suddenly unable to accept the finality of its words, the specificity, the certainty in the world being only one way and no other, but the night Edie arrived in Athens she felt an immediate reassertion of the Paraclete in her mind, a wild and almost constant whisper, and for all four months that fall and winter she felt she was in constant conversation with God, with time, with all of history and everything that every living being had ever seen, an experience that was surprisingly quiet and led her to take long walks through the city, usually alone, while other students from her international dorm were playing drinking games with ouzo or taking day trips to the coast.

Then, in a run-down but capacious park somewhere near the Temple of Zeus on the first of November, Edie found a stray dog lying on his side, his pale fur matted gray with dirt and blood crusted around his mouth. His breath was erratic and his eyes darted around as he moaned, and as Edie knelt beside him and touched his side, she knew he was dying and began to cry. Knowing she was useless with nothing to soothe his pain, she decided to stay with him under that tree until it was over, no matter how long it took, no matter if the sun would soon start going down. Settling into a trance with the animal as dusk fell, her crying had ceased, and even that constant whisper of the Holy Spirit fell away, and she heard a voice in her mind that she immediately knew corresponded to the dog himself, a realization she took in with awe and horror. As he began to speak, he stared at Edie without blinking, and his breathing became slower and softer.

Don't you remember, Marie? That time I called you and K from Athens the night I watched the dog die—but I had to try several times, and my calling card was out of minutes—don't you remember?

But Marie didn't remember—*Are you sure I was there, too? Maybe it was just K.*

It was both of you, I know it was. You would have been in the apartment on Eleanor Street. I could barely speak—

55

Weeks later, as Marie is looking through photograph negatives from that year, she will remember exactly this day, this call (early afternoon after a sudden rainstorm had passed through), and how worried she and K had been, how the dial tone had cut in while Edie was sobbing (*I can't, I can't*), and they had no way of calling her back.

But Marie can't remember that phone call right now as Edie recounts this story of the dog and the voice—a rant, really, provoked by nothing other than Marie using the word *faith*, and Edie can't stop herself now from the desire to try to tell Marie everything she knows about faith, faith in a soul, or faith in an overall meaning of things, or faith in friendships, faith in false continuities—and didn't it seem certain that all these faiths were meant to be lost, torn apart, rebuilt—lost and found, *lost and found*, that was something the dog had told her, though the details, Edie admitted, were cloudy now.

Even as she tries to put herself back in time, Edie of course cannot recall the many physical and emotional contexts at the moment she knelt there in the dim, then the dark, talking to a dying dog. Not only that, but she can't even remember some of the most important aspects of that day, that time, the specific questions she asked that dog and the specific answers he gave, and the reason she cannot remember these details is not that time itself has fogged over the memory, but because her need for self-mythology has taken over, and when she thinks back to the young woman she was in Greece, all she remembers is the religious grief, and though it is true that

anxiety about her changing beliefs was primary among her worries the autumn she was twenty, Edie was also troubled by more mundane and juvenile things—namely by her romantic entanglements with two boys her age and the standard-issue college-junior drama that these entanglements entailed.

She had not really liked either boy, but instead felt confused about her position, in each of their lives, as a desired object. She stayed up late at night trying to pray, trying to address, in the divine gaze of God, her fear that human-on-human love was really the root of all suffering, all malaise, all bad music, all good music, all addiction, all psychological problems, all joy, all art, all laughter, all sorrow, all ecstasy, most pregnancies and therefore most human beings from the best to the worst, and therefore all global warming, all disaster, all war, all science, all art, all waste, all of us and all of it, and wasn't it true that the only way out, the only way to soberly and respectably pass your life, wasn't the only honest option to devote yourself entirely to God and nothing else, to never align yourself with something so base as another person, to avoid the distraction of heartbreak and longing and mixed feelings, to avoid romantic entanglements altogether? Or was refusing God's (perfect, but twisted, but perfect) creation a kind of sacrilege on its own?

The boys who had occasioned this line of worry were an atheist from Canada and a religious studies major from London, each of whom had asked Edie to get a drink earlier in the semester, and each of whom she had declined and suggested

they join her on one of her walks instead. After the first walk, she began to walk weekly with each of them, one on Fridays and the other on Tuesdays, long walks that were not clearly romantic or platonic, though the fact that she sometimes worried she would run into the one boy while she was with the other made it clear to her that there was some kind of indirect romance involved. The atheist tended to steer their afternoons and evenings through the anarchist neighborhood, while the religious studies major preferred the more picturesque and therefore more heavily trafficked areas. Several weeks passed and neither boy found out about the other, and nothing directly romantic transpired between either couple other than the romance of long conversations connecting their lives and opinions and experiences to the philosophy and myths they were reading in their courses—she shared a class with each of them, Philosophy of Ethics with one, Overview of Greek Mythology with the other—and Edie told each boy about the extremist religious tendencies she had as a child, and her mystical experiences in girlhood that she later recognized almost verbatim in the writings of Hildegard von Bingen, though she told the stories differently to each of them without quite realizing it. And as the weeks went on, her conversations with both boys became more intimate. She and the religious studies major debated the underlying reasons—both productive and destructive—why religious doctrine worldwide and for all of history had tried to control sexual behaviors of its believers, and the disastrous consequences this had led to, mainly for women and children but also for clergy, yet in her more risqué talks with the atheist,

they had both shared, somewhat frankly, their sexual fantasies and experiences, and though she confessed to both of
them that she was still, at twenty, somewhat shamefully, a
virgin, she had told the religious studies major this was a
lingering habit from her more directly Catholic days, while
she had told the atheist the more material reason she'd never
had sex—she had tried with her high school boyfriend, just
once, and though she had wanted to and though she felt
ready, her vagina had clenched beyond her conscious control so completely that she was mysteriously impenetrable.
The boyfriend was so stunned that he'd never spoken to her
again—worried that either it was his fault or that she was,
somehow, not entirely a girl after all, which would have explained why she was friends with all the gay kids anyway.
Edie had tried again a year later with a friend; still she was as
impassable as a wall, and she'd since given up trying. The religious studies major had been slightly disturbed by his strong
desire to take Edie's Catholic virginity as soon as possible (as
they had not so much as kissed, and she had given him no in-
dication that she was even interested in him), but the atheist
took her tale of sexual abnormality as an exciting challenge, a
sword-in-the-stone situation but rather reversed.

She had begun avoiding both boys a few days before she
found the dying dog because each boy, each still unaware of
the other, had disclosed his feelings for her in the ways he
knew how. The atheist had offered, with the assured excite-
ment of a salesman, to patiently take up the task of removing
her cumbersome virginity, while the religious studies major,

his pale face aflame, indicated that he would like to commence a proper courtship, and if at the end of the semester she wished to continue their relations, he would arrange somehow to either transfer to her college in the States or have her transferred to his school in England. Edie had had no idea how this had happened. Prior to this moment, she'd only ever had that one capricious boyfriend, and she'd never had to contend with anyone else's attention, and yet there was a simple explanation for why these two very different young men had made such plain proposals just days apart: it was her preoccupied glare, always affixed in the middle distance, that had provoked each of them to want her intense preoccupation to rest on him, to fill the void they presumed her to contain.

She skipped the following week of classes and did everything she could to meditate herself into a clarity from which she thought she might be able to perceive her true feelings for the two boys, about whom she felt neither desire nor repulsion, only a tender confusion, an unbearable neutrality that she did not trust. For days she lived on broth and olive oil and meditated in silence for hours at a time, even when her roommate passed timidly through the suite. Edie spent the rest of her time slowly walking through the most derelict places in the city. Sometimes she sat in plazas and watched old women feed the pigeons as she imagined herself shriveled and elderly, infirm, unwell—hoping that an aged vision of herself might transfer some knowledge of her current situation—and she was doing exactly that when the religious

studies major noticed her, watched her for a while, then went to her, hoping to see Edie's dour expression melt into a smile at his appearance, but she instead began sobbing, and he held her and she clutched him back, too exhausted to have any idea of where the sobbing was even coming from (though it was mostly malnourishment and exhaustion). The religious studies major held her shoulders with one arm as he wiped the tears from her face, and he had the impulse to give her a little nickname right then—*"muppet"* sprang to mind—and maybe he would have done so if the atheist had not seen them and tapped Edie's shoulder and begun to lecture her, not looking at the big pale Brit who was growing increasingly confused and sad as the future he'd been imagining—a wedding at Saint Andrew's with his family's tiara—fell away. The atheist, in a voice cold and logical, said it was clear to him now that she had, all along, wished nothing more than to emotionally if not literally castrate him, that she probably had been taking this guy on walks, too, hadn't she? *She has*, the religious studies major managed, and soon the three had dispersed, all of them sickened in their own particular ways.

That was the day Edie found the dying dog, and though she has forgotten those boys completely now and may never remember them again—one was named Chris and the other Thomas—the sensation of kneeling beside the dying dog is still vivid in her mind: taking in his awful smell, the texture of sand and pebble on her knees, every cell in her body animated completely with a quaking sensation she knew to be divine ekstasis. But she still recalls the day at a slant, remembering

only her spiritual worries, and nothing of those ignoble boy troubles.

Is love human? Edie had asked the dog.

No.

Can humans love? she asked, rewording the question as if shaking the eight ball once more.

Not really. Humans have needs and when their needs are met, sometimes they call it love.

But what is love?

Me.

A dog is love?

Not all dogs. Just me in particular.

And when you die?

When I die I won't be dead.

It almost seemed that the dog smiled when he said this, that he knew something Edie could never imagine knowing.

How does someone know if they love someone? Edie asked.

God speaks clearly, despite not existing.

So if God is love, then you are God, but God doesn't exist—

There is nothing to learn from dying dogs.

But why are you speaking to me?

Men were created in order to destroy everything, and women were created so there would be one thing they couldn't destroy.

And that's the only sentence Edie now remembers the dog saying clearly, and she repeats it to Marie as she finishes gluing the teacup back together. *Men were created in order to destroy everything, and women were created so there would be one thing they couldn't destroy.* And the teacup sits there in the grim lighting, redeemed save for a few veins where it can't quite rejoin itself.

Wise dog, Marie says, *if a bit reductive and dramatic,* and now that Edie's story is over, it occurs to Marie that she is going to need to stay awake until, at least, something happens next door—until she hears someone leave or enter the apartment, until someone discovers the body that is surely emitting the blood, until a cop or a detective shows up, until there are sirens, maybe, a knock at her door, maybe, some simple questions, and even if none of this happens tonight, even if no one finds the body until tomorrow or the next day or whatever, she knows there is no way that she's going to be able to sleep

until something happens, until something is known, until the narrative that began when she saw the blood concludes with answers, an ending, a tension released.

Let's stay up, Marie says to Edie, her tone entirely new, her eyes bright and almost panicked as she refills the caballitos with mezcal again.

I already had some, Edie says, staring at the neat glass of clear liquid before her.

It's Christmas.

Marie looks the other way as she says this, as if speaking to someone else, or as if she's alone. She moves toward the window and looks down to see the women are still out there. Ripped wrapping paper and sparkling red ribbon litter the sidewalk. One of them whips a Hoola-Hoop around her waist while another two leap across an oversized hopscotch chalked in the center of the street. A few others throw paper airplanes and try to catch them. They're all laughing and laughing, then there's a kind of screaming laughter as a woman runs from an alleyway, pulling up her underwear and pushing down her skirt, having pissed in the shadows. The Hoola-Hooper lights a cigarette without stopping her spin. One streetlight is flickering while another is bright and pale orange. The giddiness of the women reverberates between and against the buildings, vibrates upward to Marie's apartment window. Has she ever seen anything more perfect

and strange? It's been an unseasonably warm December, but the holidays came anyway, talk of nuclear war in the news, people destroyed by grief, and in the dark there were grown women, barefoot, behaving like girls who'd never heard a word of it.

Edie rests her chin on Marie's shoulder, and it is a fact that when one living thing puts their chin on another living thing, everything is fine. Then Edie straightens up, cheers her glass to Marie's—*to them*, nodding out the window—and pours half of it into her mouth.

Two of the women in the street catch sight of Edie and Marie watching them from above, and almost immediately each of the women pulls down her neckline, baring her tits in the catastrophic weather. A rallying cry takes over, then the other women soon follow suit, one tit or both, some throwing the middle finger while a woman in a red dress does a cartwheel, missing her footing, falling to the ground in a fit of convulsing laughter, and who wouldn't want to be alive in a world, Marie asks herself, where such things are possible?

Edie raises her glass to the Bacchae, and they all start screaming *Merry Christmas, Happy New Year*, and Marie tips her imaginary hat at them, and after that Edie and Marie are no longer spectators, so they retreat into their beaten chairs, to their mezcal, to their worries, to their much quieter gathering, this revelry carrying on in the background.

What else did the dog tell you, Marie asks, kidding a little in a way Edie doesn't notice, *and what else did you ask? I've always wanted to talk to a dog.*

Edie tries to remember for a minute, then all at once she does—*I asked him why suffering existed, and he told me he had chosen to suffer.*

But that didn't answer your question, Marie interrupts, but Edie keeps on.

And I asked him why he had chosen to suffer, and he said that all life required it, and he had chosen to be alive, therefore he had chosen this pain. And I asked him if everyone chose to be alive, and he said no, that some people and some animals are here against their wishes, but that eventually they either come around or get out.

Grim.

And I asked him if there was an afterlife—oh, I remember this part, Edie says, interrupting her remembering to notice it—*He said the afterlife didn't come after, that it was during and before, but never after, and that this was a misunderstanding that people kept clinging to—the obsession with what comes after when there isn't an after. Just a before.*

Marie doesn't want to say it, though she also wants to say it, though she also does not, but she gives in. *But obviously . . .*

well, I mean clearly, Edie, the dog wasn't speaking to you. It was you—you were thinking those things.

Well—it's possible, but, no. I don't think so.

You told me it was a hard time—that you wanted to believe in God but didn't anymore, that you—

The dog was the one who saved me then. I don't know what I would have done if he hadn't spoken to me. I needed it.

Exactly. You needed to hear something that no one was going to tell you, so you told yourself. I don't know why you don't want to see it that way—there's nothing wrong with it. There's nothing wrong with inventing a story to explain something real to yourself.

Edie looks down and stops talking, as she doesn't want to get into a conversation with Marie or anyone about the ontological nature of the universe and the limits of perception and the uselessness of the kind of certainty that Marie is trying to force onto her memory of the dog, the voice, the experience of being near a kind of knowledge, even though she does know that the voice both was and was not her own, and also was and was not the dog, that the voice was a part of the context in which the voice first came to her, and she also knows—though she won't try to convince Marie of it—that there are different kinds of knowledge available, ambient, chaotic, at all the right and wrong times in our limited, human lives.

Two houseflies, one mounted upon the other, thrash around in what looks like rape on the arm of Edie's chair, and both women watch them struggle for a few seconds during which Edie reflexively remembers the accusations that had been made against her ex by some of his current and former students, two of them officially lodged, the other two just rumored, and how the first week she moved in with him he'd told her—disclosed, really—about the two hearings he'd had with the school in the prior year, how both those girls had been dismissed as crazy, really truly unwell, both of them having imagined conversations and encounters with him, promises he'd made, *and it was tragic really*, he'd told Edie, *tragic how real it was to them, how powerful an imagination can be.* Yet even in their deluded states, he had explained to Edie, it was interesting that neither of those women had hallucinated an overt coercion, just his attention, his love, an exaggeration, surely, of the way he taught with such intensity and kindness and clarity, how his classrooms were totally absent of authority and most students weren't used to that, being treated with that much respect by a teacher. And when he told Edie about the hearings, he also confessed that a few years back, in a moment of emotional weakness and loneliness, after his first wife had left him, he had gotten into a brief but entirely consensual relationship with one of his *former* students, but she practically forced it upon him, he'd had no choice but to give in for a little while. *I was afraid of what she might do to herself if I rejected her*, he had said, and Edie asked how old she'd been. *Twenty-three, I think.* (He was adding two years.) And how old had he been? *Thirty-five, thirty-six.*

Edie had been in love with him, but even so she couldn't stop a look of slight horror from leaking out of her eyes, and he had lectured her for this look of disdain and judgment—she had no right to judge him, and it had been so much more complicated than it may have seemed from the outside, from a distance, and she was being simply puritanical about the age difference—but a month after Edie had left him for good she'd gotten a call from an unknown number, and it was his ex-student-girlfriend explaining what had happened, which did not align with the story she'd been told. *He is so convincing, isn't he?* the woman had said. The former student and girlfriend knew, also, about the relationships he'd had before and after her, and she had a suspicion that even those women who'd been dismissed as crazy may not have been so crazy before they met him. *His class on portraiture was extremely intimate*, the woman said, *and now that I'm closer to the age he was when we began our relationship, I can see how the whole thing was really about power, and he should have known that. I wanted to be with him, but . . . The whole thing was so damaging for me, though I'm sure he would reject that idea.* Edie thanked the woman (but what for?) and hung up the phone.

Edie had often joked when they were together that she was getting a PhD in Him—that he'd told her what to think, what to read, what and whom to give her attention, the qualities that made art worthwhile, the qualities that made life worthwhile. And she had, she knew, benefited from his education. She had been improved. Yet he'd also built up in her an indestructible confidence similar to his own, had taught her to

respect herself and her ideas so much so that she, years later and slowly, began to see, through a lens he'd given her, his total disrespect of her, despite his love, the way he saw her as a project of his, a savage mind he was civilizing.

Months after she'd left him, late at night on that island in Greece, Brenda had asked Edie a question to which Edie already knew the answer, though she did not want to hear herself say it. *It's not important for you to wonder why he is the way he is anymore. What you need to ask yourself is—why were you there?*

As the two houseflies briefly struggle against each other, tumble and crash, then part, Marie, however, is thinking of nothing but the blood. One of the houseflies lands again on the arm of Edie's chair and sets to washing its hands. Marie bolts upright and goes to the squint.

Are you waiting on someone? Edie asks.

No. I just—I thought I heard something. I keep hearing things, don't you?

I don't think so. Like what things?

This building is just really fucked up, isn't it?

Marie keeps looking with one eye through this tiny window. It seems the blood puddle is still there, a little larger, maybe, or maybe it's just the distortion of the convex lens.

What do you mean "fucked up"?

The kinds of things that could happen here, you know?

But we're in here, we're fine. Door's locked. We're OK, right?

Yeah. Yes, I think so. Marie doesn't know why she can't or hasn't yet told Edie about the blood as she walks slowly back toward the living room. Marie has a vague feeling that she is somehow implicated in the existence of the blood, that her proximity to it is somehow causal, or that every moment of her inaction since she first saw the blood has accumulated into a terrible action now.

Maybe we should go to sleep soon? Edie asks, yawning, but Marie has stepped backward, unthinking, to the squint.

What are you looking at?

I don't know, Marie says. She is crying though she is not crying.

Edie goes to Marie, stands beside her at the door.

Is something out there?

No, Marie says.

Edie unlocks each lock and opens the door as Marie steps back, hoping in opposing directions—wanting so much for

the whole thing to have been a mirage while also hoping it is real and really there, a puddle of real blood, that she's not losing it again. Marie's hope is so strong she is praying without quite realizing it.

What is that? Edie asks.

By the door? In the hall?

Wait—is it . . . And Edie takes a step forward and bends toward the dark puddle. It's the length of two bodies away. *It looks like blood?*

But you said it looked like paint when you got here? Marie asks.

No, yeah—but . . . did you know it was there?

Edie can hear the women in the street begin to sing a Christmas carol as she turns to look at Marie, who can hear nothing but the beating of her own heart in her eardrums, then both of them hear another door in the hallway opening and Edie, now feeling somehow at fault or simply afraid, slams the door shut and locks it.

Neither woman moves. They each grip the other at the elbows. Each holds her breath. There are footsteps, moving and pausing, moving and pausing. Then there's a knock at the door and Marie leans to see who it is so slowly, Edie wonders

if she'll ever get there. Another knock, and now Marie sees it's the guy in 510, his cherubic face looking concerned, holding one hand with the other.

As Marie opens the door, Edie moves behind her.

There's this . . . blood, I think? He gestures toward it. *Next door?*

I saw it.

You saw it?

I thought I was having a hallucination.

A hallucination?

I didn't think it was there. I wasn't sure if it was there or not.

You have these often?

All at once Marie realizes she is exactly the kind of person who lives in this kind of building, and her neighbor, he couldn't be twenty, will likely move on to other, better places.

They come and go, she says. *There's so much you can't be sure of.*

Don't you think we should tell someone?

About the hallucinations? I have.

No, about the . . . like, blood? I knocked on their door but no one answered. It doesn't seem like anyone's in there.

That's one way to put it, Marie says, but her neighbor is silent, waits for her to explain.

Well, I'm calling 911, he says, walking away almost immediately, not even turning his head to look at the blood again.

Good idea, she says to his back.

Marie shuts and locks the door again.

He's calling 911, she tells Edie.

Oh.

Marie stands there for long enough that Edie asks her if she's OK. She is not OK. She says, *I'm OK.*

They walk away from the door very slowly, neither of them able to think of anything, neither of them able to even worry or feel dread. Someone's calling 911. An emergency has happened, but the night is so quiet, so still. They can hear women singing and laughing in the street. They sit in their chairs, the same ones, as if they can't change anything about this night now.

Do you remember that time we were walking home together—you and K and me—and that drunk guy on Smith Street called us dykes or something, then started following us—

I remember, Edie says, though she doesn't want to remember.

He was so wasted he could barely walk, remember? But he wouldn't leave us alone, and it happened so fast, K running at him and beating the shit out of that guy, right there in front of us, and I can't remember if we said anything—if you or I said anything to K. Did we say they should stop? Did we say anything?

Both Edie and Marie recall the force and flex in K's arm as it tossed the man's head against the sidewalk and the spurt of blood and the sound of his whimpering, pleading. All three of them ran, though no one and nothing was chasing them, more afraid but also more in love with K, supplicated, in need, in fear. K's white T-shirt splattered with red. K's total lack of remorse. Back at home in their bathroom K said, *I will never let anyone hurt you*, as hydrogen peroxide hissed in their knuckle gashes. Neither Edie nor Marie says anything as this memory forms and dissipates in their silence.

It was awful, Edie says, the simplest possible summary.

Sirens cut into the night and the women in the street are still laughing, and one of them starts harmonizing a howl with the sirens that grow stronger and louder until they're here,

they're right here—two cop cars parking and an ambulance coming around the corner.

Marie pours another shot of mezcal, and Edie thinks about how, of all the ways her Christmas could have gone, this wasn't one she had imagined.

Soon there are noises and voices in the hallway. Marie and Edie don't leave their chairs for some time, then Marie can't help but look out the lens in the door—several cops, crime scene tape, and it's so strange when life looks like the movies, how hard it is to live instead of act at times like that.

Marie keeps watching as Edie asks, *What is it, what's happening?* and Marie doesn't answer, which suits Edie just fine as she doesn't really want to know what it is or what is happening, as she feels sure that Marie shouldn't be living here, that K and Marie and Edie should all be together, as they were, an unbroken team facing the inexplicable and constant narrative of being alive. Both women, without knowing it, are having the same thought: K would know exactly what to do in this situation.

The woman being escorted out of the apartment by two uniformed men is wearing a white T-shirt and dark jeans, the same clothes K was wearing that night on Smith Street, just such a shirt, just such jeans; then Marie looks down at her own body to see the same white cotton and dark denim. Common clothes. Common enough. And her shirt's clean

and the woman between those two men—it seems her shirt is clean, too. Marie backs away from the door, goes to wash her hands in the bathroom without knowing why.

Then there's a knock at the door, a voice announcing himself, a voice of authority, a voice here to clean everything up, put everything back where it should be. Marie opens the door but looks past the man speaking, looks past him even as she speaks back. She's watching the woman in the white T-shirt standing between the two men as they wait for the elevator, and now the woman is turning to look at Marie, her face a little shocked and gaunt, one eye blackened with a bruise. Her white shirt, and her dark jeans, loose, and her bare feet. Why didn't they let her put on shoes?

Now Marie is making eye contact with the cop. Now she's playing nice. *Have you met your neighbors, ma'am, do you know their names, did you hear anything in the past few days from the neighboring apartment, anything strange, anything out of the ordinary?* But no, she didn't know them, no, she didn't hear anything, no, she wasn't listening, no, she didn't see anything, doesn't know anything, doesn't anything, anything. But she invites the cop in for a cup of tea. The logic of the mezcal has taken over.

This is Edie. She's heartbroken.

I'm fine, Edie says.

She's suffering, Marie clarifies. *It's very hard for her to acknowledge it.*

Marie tells the cop everything she knows, which is almost nothing. She repeats herself, she is unsteady on her feet, she is both frantic and unhurried, vaguely guilty, vaguely aloof, but by the time she pours boiling water into the teacup already on the table and watches dumbly as it sieves through the cracks, it's clear the cop has to take her in, useless as it may be; what a building, what a place, what a character, what a mess.

Edie, alone now, looks down at the street, waiting to see Marie leave the building with the cop. And there's Marie now. Goodbye, Marie. From the way she's walking, you'd think she's having a great time. The story about her weird affair hadn't made it seem like Marie was truly guilty of anything, but the sight of her getting into a police car does. Right before she closes the door behind herself, she waves to Edie like everything's totally fine, then Edie watches the car drive down the street until it turns a corner and can't be seen anymore.

The Bacchae have retired from their antics and are now sitting on the curb, sharing three cigarettes between the ten of them.

Now there's a body being carried out on a stretcher, zipped in a black shroud. The paramedics slide it into the ambulance,

and the ambulance leaves with none of the urgency of its arrival.

Through the walls, Edie can hear all the activity of the people next door, detectives, photographers, all the people that have to be gathered in order to discern the recent history of that room, looking for the blame, hunting for it like children playing an orderly and gruesome game.

Edie unlocks the door and cracks it open, listening to and watching the men moving with careful authority in and out of the apartment and the men standing in the hallway, some thumbing at their phones, some filling out forms, some doing nothing but squinting in the fluorescents. None see her until one of them does.

What happened? she asks him.

Of course I can't tell you that, the detective says. *But I can tell you*—and he lowers his voice now and comes closer to her—*that body had been in there for maybe two days, heart attack seems like, but with a head wound from the fall, and the girlfriend*—he lowers his voice even more, comes even closer—*she didn't do anything. Didn't call anyone. Didn't try to help. She just watched the fucker die.*

Oh, Edie says.

Dark shit. The things people will do.

From the way he is looking at her, Edie knows it is time to shut the door again and lock it. She doesn't even say good-bye or thank you or good luck—nothing. She just shuts the door.

Months later during the trial the woman will testify that she cannot remember the man's heart attack, that she cannot remember him clutching his chest or complaining of pain, that she knew he had a history of heart problems, but that she cannot remember him falling, she did not see him hit his head, she does not remember him bleeding on the floor, that she doesn't remember him asking her to call anyone, that she cannot, now, even remember what his voice sounded like. They had been living in that apartment for three years. She worked menial jobs when she could get them, and he worked in the factory across the street.

He was a nice man, the woman will say, so softly, at the trial. *I am sorry for what happened to him.*

The judge will ask her to speak up. A lawyer will ask if the man ever hit her.

I don't think so, she will say.

You were found with a black eye and bruises on your arms. Where did you get those?

I can't remember.

The public defense lawyer assigned to her case will argue she was and may still be in shock, that the state of the apartment suggested that she had barely been able to take care of herself for days, that her clothes were soaked in urine, that she was quite disoriented when she was discovered, but there was no alcohol or drugs in her bloodstream, that she is not a threat to society, that when the cops broke down her door they found her sitting near the body, reading poetry aloud to him. She seemed to believe he was listening while taking a nap.

We used to have a game—he would pretend to be dead and I would pretend not to notice. I must have thought we were playing. We knew each other so well, sometimes it wasn't clear if we were talking to each other or if I was just imagining it.

As soon as it begins, Edie and Marie will be consumed with the trial and ensuing legal purgatory, the hung juries, the arguments, the articles, all the evidence in her favor and against it, but before all that there was this—this night that Marie is at the police station being as useless as she was suspicious, telling them about how her wife kicked her out and now she almost never got to see the twins, *my children*, she manages to say, and though the cops tell her this is of no consequence, she keeps talking about how beautiful it must be to be a twin—the sense of knowing there is really a person, one particular person, who is that much a part of your life.

Or does it set an impossible precedent? Marie asks a man in front of her, entirely sober now. The sunrise is near and the shift

has changed over; a new detective has taken the other one's place, though Marie can barely tell the difference.

An impossible precedent for what? he asks.

For love.

Oh, we're talking about love, are we?

Everyone else arrives alone, but a twin comes with someone. They come with someone. That means something.

A brother or sister, sure.

But it's more than that.

Family connections are serious, yes, it's in the blood.

No—it's more than that, it's much more. There were times I held my wife and I thought it was prehistoric, that feeling, and I'd never had it with anyone else, never with my family, never even with my kids, this feeling that we came together, we went together, like we were not even people, really, but just matter, animal matter that had evolved a million years so we could just be in bed on a Saturday morning while the kids were still asleep, and we had nothing to do but smell each other . . .

The detective is trying to listen, he really is, but he has no idea what she means by "prehistoric."

And I don't know what else people are supposed to do other than have faith in each other, but I'm starting to worry it's not real, that it can really go away without warning and really be gone. Big things don't just vanish, you know? Buildings, whales, cities, old trees, you know?

Trees?

They don't vanish.

Suppose they don't.

So then if something can vanish that fast, was it real?

Is what real? The detective's curiosity is outrunning his confusion for now. Even though he doesn't understand what the question is, he wants to know the answer.

One faith goes away, and a new faith arrives, a faith that the old faith will come back or just a new faith in something else. Or is it possible that the new faith only seems to be new? It could just be the old faith, changed. Like if you went into a coma for two years and woke up and your dog had lost a leg in the meantime. New dog, but the same dog.

Marie is staring intently at the detective, thinking she's really on to something now, though she's on to nothing. She lost track of herself hours ago, and now she's just out there, saying things.

OK, well. The only thing is—what does this have to do with your neighbors?

I don't want to be doomed.

Doomed how?

When it comes to the possibility of a real faith—

The detective is giving up now, calling it a draw. It's clear the supposed witness witnessed nothing, that she's just one of those lonely people who wants to be questioned, who thinks something is going to come of it. He's sending her home, now letting her out the locked side door and locking it behind her.

Marie starts walking down the alley, immediately heading home, not looking back, none of her thinking slowed, though now she's talking only to herself instead of that man.

Back at the apartment Edie has found the voice of the dog.

How does it feel to be dead? Edie asks him as she waits for the sunrise, staring out Marie's window, wide awake.

It feels not quite as noticeable as being alive, given the lack of linear time, but it's better than dying, for quite the same reason.

And why do people want to destroy things that are beautiful?

Fear.

Fear of what?

The same thing fear is always fearing.

And what's that?

Fear.

A fear of fear?

I'm glad I was never human.

And this fear holding hands with love—is it always a fear of the end?

Edie will remember none of this.

It is, though there are all kinds of endings, all kinds of death, and none of them require fear. All death is beautiful.

Are we sure that all death is beautiful?

All death is beautiful because everything dies.

But what about the fear?

This isn't to say you shouldn't fear what is beautiful.

Should you always fear what is beautiful?

To witness beauty is to be afraid.

And so it should always be feared?

Let's not confuse being afraid with being fearful.

And so it should never be feared?

"Never" and "always" have no place here.

The voice of the dead dog fades in Edie's mind as slow morning light turns the room gray-blue. There's one week left of this year, this awful, joyful, terrifying year that has seemed to give and take so much from her.

Where were her things? Where was her life?

Then again it was just a life—a home, some people, a body, and her faith that any of those things could be relied upon indefinitely. These were more or less the same small things that comprise anyone's life, lost and gained and lost like that, endless for now but not endless, never endless.

There is no story that does not lead to another story, Edie thinks, or maybe it was the dead dog speaking again.

Which makes you wonder, then, what all these stories are for? Edie doesn't quite whisper to the empty room.

Something is happening inside Edie, something outside the reach of language, and she first thinks it must be the dog again, but it isn't the dog. It was Edie, whatever or whomever Edie is, and finally a real fact about faith is coming to her, something she wants to give to Marie once she comes home.

She sits there for a full hour as the day breaks, trembling, sleepless, one exhausted little human life just trying to live and finding it difficult. Then, as if someone else is making the decision, she stands and goes to the cupboard and chooses a beautiful gray teacup. She sets the teacup on the floor, then takes the crowbar from the wall and sets it beside the cup.

The morning is here now, indisputably here. Edie looks out the window and sees the Bacchae sleeping in a beautiful little pile in the street.

Now Marie is walking toward the building, and Edie watches her friend make her way down the sidewalk, already anxious to tell her everything she's realized in the night. She is completely certain she will never forget what she's feeling right now, and she's as right as she is wrong. She will forget it and remember it and forget it constantly, an ordinary cycle she will live with all her life, or so it seems.

Marie unlocks all the locks and the dead bolt, opens the door, then she sees it, the teacup and the crowbar and the light just so.

ACKNOWLEDGMENTS

Thank you Daniel Saldaña París, Sara Rich, Brenda Cullerton, Brenda Lozano, Sean Brennan, Callie Freeman, Kendra Malone, Maryse Meijer, Wilhelmina Peragine, Filip Tejchman, Jenny Polus, Sarah Manguso, John Vanderslice, Maria Brand, Sammy Loren, Dr. Lozano, Casa Lozano, La Casa Azul, Haroula Rose, Oliver Hill, Christian Stavros, fireplaces, firepits, a certain hammer, John Wray, Sasha Frere-Jones, Isaac Fitzgerald, Kelly Farber, Zac Rae, Amanda Yates Garcia, Kathleen Mackay, Patrick Cottrell, Geoff Dyer, Martin Pousson, Khash Khabushani, Kyp Malone, Francis Farewell Starlite, Patrick deWitt, Tron Miller, Jonathan Lethem, Sarah Ruhl, Paul Holdengräber, Karen Russell, Max Porter, Jim McManus, Emma Lirette, Linda Lirette, Deenah Vollmer, Georgia Bean, my mother, my fathers, my siblings, Chelsea Hodson, Seneca, Tabor Allen, Camila Ibarra, Persephone, Evy, nudity, La Bodega, Augustín, Brian Holder-Chow Lin On, Águila Blanca, Casa Chepil, the pigs, the goats, San Augustinillo, Playa Mermejita, the free-roaming chickens in Mazunte, Banana Bread the cat, Kit Schluter, Golden Teacher, Minhal Baig, Maria Villarreal, Aden Hakimi, U-Haul, Bad Bunny drag night at C'mon Everybody, Greene Avenue, Omi, DW Gibson, Rebecca Novack, Peter Musante, San Cristóbal, poisonous walks under Los Angeles freeways, Cuidad de México, Cuernavaca, La Pitaya, the Jan Michalski Foundation, those dozen hawks who flew outside my window one day, Jason Arthur, Eric Chinski, Jackson Howard, Jin Auh.

WORKS CONSULTED

Alien Tapes, Geo Wyeth; *All About Love*, bell hooks; *Big Time*, Angel Olsen; *The Beauty of the Husband*, Anne Carson; *Bluets*, Maggie Nelson; *Cain Named the Animal*, Shane McCrae; *The Cedars*, John Vanderslice; *Death Jokes*, Amen Dunes; *The Details*, Ia Genberg (translated by Kira Josefsson); *Directions to Myself*, Heidi Julavits; *Easy Beauty*, Chloé Cooper Jones; *Forbidden Notebook*, Alba de Céspedes (translated by Ann Goldstein); *The Freezer Door*, Matilda Bernstein Sycamore; *Gravity & Grace*, Simone Weil (translated by Emma Crawford and Mario von der Ruhr); *In Memory of Memory*, Maria Stepanova (translated by Sasha Dugdale); "In the Desert," Stephen Crane; "It's All Coming Back to Me Now," Céline Dion; *Liars*, Sarah Manguso; *Like a Sky Inside*, Jakuta Alikavazovic (translated by Daniel Levin Becker); *Like Hearts Swelling*, Polmo Polpo; *Love and Living*, Thomas Merton; *Love's Work*, Gillian Rose; *Music for Spaceships and Forests*, Twi the Humble Feather; *On Being Blue*, William Gass; *Run Towards the Danger*, Sarah Polley; *Sleepless Nights*, Elizabeth Hardwick; *Slow Focus*, Fuck Buttons; *Splinters*, Leslie Jamison; *Tonight I'm Someone Else*, Chelsea Hodson; *The Undiscovered Self*, Carl Jung; *The Undying*, Anne Boyer; *Un Verano Sin Ti*, Bad Bunny; *We've Been Going About This All Wrong*, Sharon Van Etten.

CREDITS

EDITORIAL
Eric Chinski
Jackson Howard
Brianna Fairman

REPRESENTATION AND RIGHTS
Jin Auh
Abram Scharf
Anna Haddelsey
Jessica Bullock
The Wylie Agency

TEXT DESIGN
Gretchen Achilles

JACKET DESIGN
Alex Merto

PRODUCTION MANAGER
Nina Frieman

PRODUCTION EDITORS
Carrie Hsieh
Nancy Elgin

MANAGING EDITORS
Debra Helfand
Scott Auerbach

PUBLICITY
Brian Gittis

MARKETING
Daniel del Valle
Hillary Tisman
Nicholas Stewart
Caitlin Cataffo
Sam Glatt
Jonathan Woollen
Isabella Miranda

CONTRACTS
Erika Seidman
Penny Chu

SALES
Spenser Lee

COPYEDITING
Nancy Clements

PROOFREADING
NaNá V. Stoelzle
Susan Bishansky